Disclaimer

Hi, I'm Doug Giles. Glad to meet you. What you have in your hands, Christian, is going to cause you to rock in a hard place. Yep, if you do what is written in these pages you will thrive when others quit, you will soar while others crash and burn. Not because I say so, but because these are eternal principles that the Scripture has spelled out for the saints when they get saddled with the slop of living life in a fallen, mucked-up world.

I've got to warn you about my writing style. It is brutal and loaded with heavy doses of acerbity. In this day everything smells, so I figure attitude sells. I take my cue from Ted Nugent, not Ted Haggard. Yes, this is not a PC book, but it is tasty if you like reality. It is my hope that it will make you think, make you mad, and make you laugh your butt off, but the main thing I hope it will do is make you rise up with faith instead of lie on the floor in the fetal position with life-rattling fear.

DOUG GILES

IF YOU'RE GOING THROUGH HELL, KEEP GOING!

BRIDGE
LOGOS
FOUNDATION

Alachua, Florida 32615

Bridge-Logos
Alachua, FL 32615 USA

If You're Gong Through Hell, Keep Going!
by Doug Giles

Library of Congress Catalog Card Number: 2009932776
International Standard Book Number 978-0-88270-973-4

Scripture quotations in this book marked KJV are from the *King James Version* of the Bible.

Scripture quotations marked NASB are taken from the *New American Standard Bible.* © 1960, 1962, 1963, 1968, 1971, 1972, 1973, 1975, 1977 by The Lockman Foundation. Used by permission.

Scripture quotations marked MSG are taken from *The Message.* Copyright ©1993, 1994, 1995, 1996, 2000, 2001, 2002. Used by permission of NavPress Publishing Group.

Scripture quotations marked NLT are taken from the *Holy Bible, New Living Translation,* copyright © 1996. Used by permission of Tyndale House Publishers, Inc., Wheaton, Illinois 60189. All rights reserved.

Cover graphic by Paul Hildebrand,
Hildebrand Graphics
www.HildebrandGraphics.com

G218.316.N.m908.35260

Dedication

To Wayne and Mae Woods,
in memory of their twenty-three-year-old son, Shane,
who died in Iraq serving God, his country, and
the Iraqis who longed for liberty.

GREATER LOVE HAS NO ONE THAN THIS,
THAT ONE LAY DOWN HIS LIFE FOR HIS FRIENDS.
JOHN 15:13

Contents

Foreword   xi

Introduction: If You Came to Christ to Be Problem-Free, Then You're Dumber Than a Bag of Hammers   xiii

1   A Cat 5 Hurricane is Coming Soon … to You!   1

2   Are You Gonna Cowboy Up or Lay There and Bleed?   17

3   It's About Character, Stupid   37

4   The Three Sources of "Hell"   53

5   Solomon Says, "Relax"   71

6   From Crappy to Happy   85

7   I Doubt, Therefore I'm Done   97

8   The "F" Word   113

9   In Summation   133

Foreword

Strength of character used to be a common trait in American culture. This is no longer true. The time-honored virtues of courage under trial and a tenacious spirit when pursuing noble goals has given way to convenience and compromise, and has spawned an unhealthy cowardice.

This attitude of surrendering to difficulties instead of overcoming them has crippled us personally, spiritually, and nationally. If our citizens, our houses of worship, and our God-blessed land desire to continue to be uniquely favored, then a tough hide to make right decisions and a holy resiliency to stand by such decisions is not negotiable.

Doug Giles, in this thought-provoking book, directly addresses wilting Christian doggedness, and exhorts believers to "cowboy up," be men, steel their wills, and joyfully live a robust Christian life in the face of personal, ecclesiastical, and national difficulties.

Written in conversational language (which has made Giles a popular columnist on the nation's largest conservative news portal, Townhall.com), Doug fuels his arguments for the Christian to toughen up with many Bible passages, biting humor, and uncommon common sense.

Within the covers of this book Doug explores such controversial topics as why God allows pain in our lives, why believers backslide when things become difficult, how the Church became the emasculated mess that it is, and what will happen to Christians if they stay soft. He gives insights as to how lives can be rebuilt with biblical boldness and how we can become the champions God has called us to be.

As a retired military man, I understand first-hand the importance of strength of character in bad situations and how important this virtue is when the chips are down. Well, dear reader, the chips are down in America. Our nation is getting rocked economically and socially. Since this is what we are facing as Christians and as Americans, we need the ability to keep going in a righteous direction, even when to do so means swimming against the tide.

And that is exactly what this timely and important book does. It helps you keep going in a righteous direction in the midst of hellish circumstances. It is truly a useful guide and field manual for victorious spiritual living.

Paul E. Vallely, Major General, US Army (Ret.)
Co-author of the best-selling book, *Endgame: Blueprint for Victory for Winning the War on Terror*
Chairman of the "Stand Up America Project."
http://standupamericaus.com/

Introduction

If You Came to Christ to Be Problem-Free, Then You're Dumber Than a Bag of Hammers

Tribulations cannot cease until God either sees us remade or sees that our remaking is now hopeless. —C.S. Lewis

These things I have spoken unto you, that in me ye might have peace. In the world ye shall have tribulation; but be of good cheer, I have overcome the world. (John 16:33, kjv)

One of the main things that I like about the Jesus of Scripture (aside from Him saving me from being deep-fried in sulfur and stuff) is this: He didn't pawn flapdoodle off on His friends, followers, or foes. He told them the unvarnished, non-tweaked, very un-PC, straight up truth—whether folks liked it or not.

Jesus, the Warrior King, wasn't a needy, autoerotic politician who would tell you *whatever* in order to get elected. He was the Savior out to salvage dunderheads like us from temporal and eternal self-destruction. This mission of rescuing our souls from eternally roasting on Dante's Viking Grill, coupled with us having a productive schlep on this globe, required that Christ tell us the truth and not goofy fairy tales. That sounds nice and good on paper, but truth—like some girls without makeup (and some guys now!)—can be scary.

Truth was odd in Jesus' day and is even stranger in ours, and that's what makes Christ appealing, and man-pleasing bootlicks appalling—at least to me. Y'know, we love to love Jesus. However, I'm a guessin' that if Jesus were around in today's feel-good-grin-until-your-teeth-are-dried culture of "I'm okay, you're okay," we probably wouldn't like Him, and He most likely would not be hired by any of the speakeasy churches which dominate the ground across this land. He probably wouldn't get airtime on lame therapeutic Christian TV and radio nor appear on *The View* because of His reputation for brandishing a verbal hammer on people and places without giving anybody a heads up.

I believe like never before that America's GP can't handle plain dealing. I can hear Nicholson screaming now, "You want to know the truth? You can't handle the truth!" Yes, I hear voices. (Mostly high-pitched, angry Chinese voices.) Anyway, we have officially become wussies with a capital W when it comes to hearing what we need to hear versus what we want to hear. Reality makes our tummies hurt. We *say* we want the truth and love the truth, but when it comes to the stuff that applies to our lives, we'd appreciate the sword's edge being dulled a bit, thank you.

Even though this penchant for being pampered is more egregious in our day, this is nothing new. The Apostle Paul warned his first mate Timothy in the first century about such a funk in Ephesus among religious wonks who wouldn't listen, read, watch, download, or tithe to anything which didn't stroke their soft underbelly.

Check out his words to Timothy:

I can't impress this on you too strongly. God is looking over your shoulder. Christ himself is the Judge, with the final say on everyone, living and dead. He is about to break into the open with his rule, so proclaim the Message with intensity; keep on your watch. Challenge, warn, and urge your people. Don't ever quit. Just keep it simple. You're going to find that there will be times when people will have no stomach for solid teaching, but will fill up on spiritual junk food—catchy opinions that tickle their fancy. They'll turn their backs on truth and chase mirages. But you—keep your eye on what you're doing; accept the hard times along with the good; keep the Message alive; do a thorough job as God's servant. (2 Timothy 4:1-5, MSG)

In contrast to the ear-ticklers Timothy had to field, Christ, who is the way, *the truth,* and the life, didn't trade in bunkum. He said it's the truth that will set you free and sometimes, most times, that truth is more uncomfortable to our me-monkey psyches than being constipated during a Celine Dion concert. Being constipated is bad enough. Being constipated *and* having to listen to Celine Dion for two hours … plus an encore … brutal. Kill me now, Lord.

The scriptural blurb from the Gospel of John with which I opened this chapter, for example, states that Christ promised His chosen disciples, His boys, His *hombres,* His *amigos,* that they would go through "hell." Not literally, but figuratively. He said, "… ye shall have tribulation." My translation in the King Doug Contra Mundus Version of the Bible is this: "Sometimes, boys, in this life, things are gonna suck and suck bad. Really bad. I'm talking worse than an airplane toilet."

The Son of God didn't Lysol the fact that if you cast your lot with Him that it'll cost you. He told them truth. He warned them that trouble was coming their way. And not just a little pinch, but rather major pain on the tribulation-size scale. For you junk food eaters, that would be super-sized problems.

He didn't exempt His mates from pain as some kind of celestial perk just because they believed in Him, but rather assured them that pressure, oppression, tribulation, affliction, and dire straits we're coming to a theater near them. But He also told them not to sweat it because in Him they were going to be able to tap into unshakable assurance, deep peace, and serious *cojones* while the unwashed masses simply flapped about. That's all He promised them. Which ain't bad, mind you.

Compare that 411 of promised pain that Christ hit His disciples with to the la-di-da painless, be a better you, positive, twenty-four/seven sunshine and birds chirpin' smack doled out by mega-churches most of the time. You'd think by listening to these ministers of misinformation and half-truths that coming to Christ exempts you from the excrement of life. I'd love it if all the cheery little ditties these televangelists proclaim *were* true and all I had to do was just believe in Jesus, be positive, and my life would turn into a lite beer commercial. But the fact of the matter is that following Christ is brutal. I suggest if you chose, or rather get chosen, to be on His team that you put on a cup.

Because Christ gave His guys the heads up that they could possibly lose everything from their reputations to their lives, the original twelve were a tad pluckier than our current pusillanimous pack. The first-century boys heard from the horse's mouth, no offense, Lord, that bovine scat would be par for their course. This had a toughening effect upon their hides. Yep, you do not read about these gents making mountains out of molehills, squealing about their pinched flesh, becoming atheists when they didn't get a new squeaky toy, or lying on the counselor's couch for ten years because Bartholomew made fun of their haircuts.

What you do see is the early Church embracing unbelievable difficulties, persevering under insane trials, laughing their butts off when they should have been crying, glorifying God when most folks today would be cussin' Him out, and radically growing both qualitatively and quantitatively, when most Christians would have laid down and died.

I'm here to tell you, ladies and gents, that the early Church had a moxie that the twenty-first-century squirrelly Church desperately needs. It appears that a theology of internal and external pain put to the original Ichthus crowd helped them to sail through the slop life saddled them with, and they became better and not bitter because of it.

Imagine that. Growth through pain.

Chapter One

A Cat 5 Hurricane is Coming Soon ... to You!

GOD WHISPERS TO US IN OUR PLEASURES, SPEAKS TO US
IN OUR CONSCIENCE, BUT SHOUTS IN OUR PAINS: IT IS HIS
MEGAPHONE TO ROUSE A DEAF WORLD. —C.S. LEWIS

First impressions are huge. When I draft a column or queue up for my radio show I know that every week (with my column) and each day (with my show) that I am picking up new readers or listeners and, being the conscientious guy that I am, I want to make sure that I make a good impression upon them.

That's why I berate my editor like I do.

I know it doesn't sound Christ-like, but there is a reason why I keep (let's call him "Andrew") in a dimly lit, unventilated, dank room underneath my stairs, sparsely fed, hydrated only on old, hot brewsky, and grossly underpaid. I want excellence. I want quality. I want control. An impression must be made, and dang it, I'll Gitmo whomever I must to get it.

Call me weird, but I quite fancy a grammatically brilliant, factually accurate column for my crowd, and if he doesn't provide that, then he gets the leaded green garden hose. You don't want the green garden hose, trust me. Only, and I mean only, when he delivers utter perfection do I let him out in the yard for a quick cable run and some sun.

As stated, I take first impressions seriously.

My editor must, I said *must*, make me look good and read good, or is it goodly or goodish? Anyhoo, the point is "Andrew" must make me rock; he must perfect my voice, not only because of unbridled self-love and obsession, but principally because I want to leave my *nuevo* readers with an unmistakable stamp when they have the good fortune of landing on my imbalanced screeds at www.TownHall.com.

In addition, I'm freakishly fastidious with not only the content and delivery of my world-famous talk show, but with the show flow itself. If you don't believe me, ask the board operators who run my program at IRN/USA Radio Network. They hate me.

Why doth they hateth me?

There are many reasons, but it is essentially because of the first impression thang.

Yep, all my cues, prompts, musical beds, and segues must be flawless or else heads will be severed from bodies, children will be left fatherless, anthrax will be mailed to grandmothers, and dogs will be poisoned. Just kidding about poisoning the dogs.

Again, why do I keeve to such an extent? I am out to impress, to mark, to scar, to brand, and to cut into my fresh new fans' flesh as to who I am, what I'm about, and what they can expect from me and my weird pen and microphone.

Behold … the importance of first impressions.

Jesus Didn't Mumble

The first impression/opening major message, at least according to Matthew's gospel, that Christ doled out to the first century dolts namely, the Sermon on the Mount (SOM), is … uh … kind of important given that it's the initial main teaching that tumbled off His tongue.

Yep, this sermon was the course setter; for you NASCAR enthusiasts I guess it would be the pace car of what it means to be a Christian. This is what Christ's kitchen will be cooking. This is it, man. Jesus is delivering His guts, making His mark on what it means to be a believer. These are not timid suggestions or faint hints as to what one should expect from His pierced hands. This is the real deal and if you don't like it you might want to take your whiny, goggle-eyed, narcissistic, chunky butt from His presence and go worship Buddha or Carrot Top.

This massive three chapter lecture series was His rabbinic coming out party. God, the Father, was showcasing His Son, making His first impression, telling all people within earshot, and throughout time immemorial what to expect if they were to hang with Him.

For example: just a scant glance of the first twelve verses of the SOM hammers home very clearly to this thick-headed author what Christ likes and by implication, what He no likey. Remember, this ain't fluff, folks, that Jesus is peddling. This is Christ's primary, at least according to Matthew, major roll-out of how He rolls and if we don't get it, it isn't because He didn't make it crystal clear; it's because we aren't listening, or we're stubborn monkeys, or we're just plain straight-up, dog-eared stupid.

Take for instance Jesus' opening volley—the Beatitudes.

When Jesus saw His ministry drawing huge crowds, He climbed a hillside. Those who were apprenticed to Him, the committed, climbed with Him. Arriving at a quiet place, He sat down and taught His climbing companions. This is what He said:

You're blessed when you're at the end of your rope.
With less of you there is more of God and his rule. You're

blessed when you feel you've lost what is most dear to you. Only then can you be embraced by the One most dear to you. You're blessed when you're content with just who you are—no more, no less. That's the moment you find yourselves proud owners of everything that can't be bought. You're blessed when you've worked up a good appetite for God. He's food and drink in the best meal you'll ever eat. You're blessed when you care. At the moment of being "care-full," you find yourselves cared for. You're blessed when you get your inside world—your mind and heart—put right. Then you can see God in the outside world. You're blessed when you can show people how to cooperate instead of compete or fight. That's when you discover who you really are, and your place in God's family. You're blessed when your commitment to God provokes persecution. The persecution drives you even deeper into God's kingdom. Not only that—count yourselves blessed every time people put you down or throw you out or speak lies about you to discredit me. What it means is that the truth is too close for comfort and they are uncomfortable. You can be glad when that happens—give a cheer, even!—for though they don't like it, I do! And all heaven applauds. And know that you are in good company. My prophets and witnesses have always gotten into this kind of trouble. (Matthew 5:1-12, MSG)

In the first chunk of the SOM we see Jesus make a clean break from the religious mooks of His day with what we church folks call "the Beatitudes." That's a twenty-dollar word for attitudes and actions that God likes, which, if you by His power, do them, God calls you blessed or in our vernacular, a "lucky dog."

Why is one fortunate if he or she takes on these seven divine ditties?

4

This, too, is easy algebra.

It is because God's fond of them and He can kill you, so you might want to put on your taps and dance to them, 007, that's why.

These are not suggestions, Ms. Postmodern Relativistic Pseudo Saint. These are facts, Jack. You remember facts, don't you? You don't? Take some meds; maybe then you'll remember. Christ is telling His posse, " … be/do this and you're blessed." By implication what does it also mean? Don't do this and you are … you are … uh … what's the opposite of blessed?

Uh … uh … um … uh … is it cursed?

Yes!

You're right.

Pat yourself on the head and eat a dog biscuit because you connected the divine dots and you got the message that Christ wanted you to get, i.e., there's a blessed way and there is a brutal, sucky, cursed way, *capice*? Yep, sweet and cuddly 7 pound, 13 ounce baby Jesus pronounced benedictions and maledictions straight out of the ministerial gate. What's the initial impression meta-tagged to the inquirer? If we wanna be blessed, do Heaven's X-Y-Z and if we wanna be cursed … don't do them.

Pretty simple, eh?

First impressions.

[Author's note: I know the Beatitudes sound poetic and very *Precious Moments* figurine-ish, but make no mistake about it—these attitude actions were so contrary to the crowd He rattled them off to, that they sought to kill Him. And if I remember correctly, I believe they eventually did.]

Moving quickly from the "blessed" list, Jesus starts informing folks about what His disciples would be in the world, namely light and salt (Matthew 5:1-16). That's illumination and preservation to a crud-addled culture. If they were not light and salt, they were to be thrown on a manure pile and trampled underfoot by men. That ain't nice.

Thirdly, we see Jesus laying down what the law truly meant and not just what the letter advocated or forbade (Matthew 5:17-48). Impression? Just because one hasn't literally committed the physical act of adultery, Christ still considers chronic masturbation as pretty much the same thing as infidelity. Roger that?

Fourthly, we see Jesus steering His boys away from making a big deal about giving money to charity, being holy just to impress stupid humans, and the proper way to pray to our Father "who art in Heaven" (Matthew 6:1-15). Impression? He hates hypocrites and God is to be approached in prayer properly.

Fifthly, Jesus, just to make sure we didn't miss it in His last exhortation, replows the point about doing your acts of worship for God and not for the applause of men (Matthew 6:16-24). Impression? See above.

Sixthly, in Matthew 6:25-34, we see Christ flying in the face of the faithless and feckless "believers" who sweat the small stuff and cannot believe that God will take care of them even though He takes care of sparrows and flowers. Impression? Unbelief is insulting and ridiculous.

Seventhly, Christ fish-slaps the upright citizen brigade, y'know ... the God Squad who rabidly judge other people without first judging themselves (Matthew 7:1-6). Sorta like one preacher did in 2006, warning us all about the peril of Brad and Chad getting it on while he's buying meth and bumping uglies with a male prostitute. Impression? We're all sinfully ridiculous and should tiptoe around lambasting fellow mortals or we could find ourselves buying meth and having sex with male prostitutes. Note that.

Eighthly, Jesus sends out another exhortation to pray in Matthew 7:7-12. Impression? I wonder ...

Ninthly, He hammers home to us that it is possible to think we're going to Heaven when, in fact, we're on the highway to

6

hell (Matthew 7:13-23). Impression? Uh, serious spiritual self-examination.

So far we've seen what is "blessed" in God's eyes, how His disciples are to be in the world, Jesus' laws for relationships, what He says about cash, prayer, fasting, judging others, the proper way to pray, the stairway to Heaven, and the highway to hell.

Ladies and gents, He's been incredibly plain in what He and the other two Persons of the Godhead expect of us critters. He's laying it down thick, Sling Blade. Are you getting this?

If a person after hearing Jesus' SOM thinks they can worship cash, pray to the Devil, indulge the superfluity of naughtiness twenty-four/seven and not be considered an adulterer, and that it is okay to be a faithless worrywart, they have clearly not gotten the impression Christ was trying to make in His opening message and are about as sharp as a bag of wet mice.

As stated, He's laying it down. The question is ... are we picking it up?

Some of you are, no doubt, wondering what all of the above has to do with the topic of this book. Settle down. I'm not finished with my ham-fisted, fly-over of the SOM.

There's a little chunk left that I haven't touched yet, so cool your jets.

Christ has a finale, a summation, and a *coup de grace* for the carnal mind. For you Springer devotees, it's kind of like Jerry's final thought for the show. There is one more thing that He wants to tattoo on His follower's soul before He and the boys go to The Olive Garden for soup and salad and the house *vino*.

What do you think the concluding topic is?

Perhaps, a discourse on the felicitous state of Heaven where one day the redeemed will sit on clouds, wearing white *peignoirs*, and walking around with glazed eyes, singing Enya songs forever and ever?

God, I hope not. That sounds like hell to me. But I digress.

The answer to that question would be, H to the no.

Is it another message about money?

Wrong again, Creflo Dollar, so relax, sit down, and put your eyes back in their sockets.

No, Christ's *précis* that He wants to impress upon those who are about to buy His T-shirts is this: both the righteous and the wicked will experience storms. You might call it pain, or crap, or BS, or gobbledygook, or problems, or junk, or crud. Whatever you wish to dub the bad stuff, it's unmistakable that Christ told us all, upfront, that the storms of life will hit both the Billy Grahams and the Billy Idols.

I know, I hate that 411 also, but it does, finally, bring me up to speed with the topic of this book.

Riders on the Storm

These words I speak to you are not incidental additions to your life, homeowner improvements to your standard of living. They are foundational words, words to build a life on. If you work these words into your life, you are like a smart carpenter who built his house on solid rock. Rain poured down, the river flooded, a tornado hit— but nothing moved that house. It was fixed to the rock. But if you just use my words in Bible studies and don't work them into your life, you are like a stupid carpenter who built his house on the sandy beach. When a storm rolled in and the waves came up, it collapsed like a house of cards. (Matthew 7:24-27, MSG)

In Jesus' first meet-and-greet He branded His believers, right off the bat, with the promise of pain. Storms for everyone! We will all go through hell. Not literal hell, but pain-in-the-butt hell. I know this information is wedging sideways with some. They're thinking ...

Storms?

At the hand of God?

WTH?

No, thank you.

That ain't right.

My grinning, cheesy, over-moussed minister who puts the "gel" in evangelical never told me that smack.

"God would never allow His precious ones to go through a hellacious storm, would He? I understand God giving the blunt end of the pool cue to the overtly impious, rebellious rats that whizz on His commandments, but Christians too? What kind of thank you is that for following His commands and listening to Christian rock? That's no way to treat your friends, Yahweh. No wonder not too many people are lining up to follow You nowadays," thus saith the Mariah Carey, self-obsessed, me-monkey kind of Christian.

Sorry for the dig, Mimi.

Now, contrary to the American Crapola Gospel peddled by tawdry pseudo-Christian hucksters on TV, Jesus promised not only puppy dogs and candy canes for Christians, but He also promised life-razing storms.

Yeah ... He assured us of bad hooey.

Matter of fact, when the Son of God chose an image to give the sense of what He was forewarning His followers about, He used three metaphors so that it would be unmistakable what kind of bovine scat they should brace for—namely, rains, floods, and winds that are so violent that if our "house" isn't built well, well ... we're screwed.

Now, most of us would like to think that the righteous would get a reprieve from pain, but to do so will make us as wrong as Blagojevich is shady and snake-eyed.

Storms Suck

I've spent all my life in two deadly storm-riddled area codes—the 806 and the 305—West Texas and South Florida, respectively. In West Texas it was tornadoes. In South Florida it's hurricanes. Having experienced both these death-dealers, all I've got to say is … I prefer a hurricane to a tornado.

Tornadoes are like Jesus. They show up when you're not expecting them. Anyone who has spent anytime living in tornado alley knows exactly what I'm talking about.

You West Texas ladies know what I'm talkin' about, don't you? Y'know, you're driving your kids to school in your Escalade and as you're tooling along putting on eye liner with one hand, texting with the other, typing on your laptop with your left foot, and writing a note with your mouth, you glance up and notice clouds building up in the west-north-west, which means that you might get some rain later on in the afternoon.

No biggee.

The storm looks several hours away.

No cause for alarm.

So, as usual, you drop your rug rats off at prison, I mean public school, and customarily, after your morning errands, you head off to Starbucks for your ritual half-decaf, skinny, frappachino with spiced, spider monkey milk, and to meet your lover, sorry, your *prayer partner*, named Todd, who is rabidly metrosexual, lactose intolerant, and sports a pinky ring.

As you're walking across the parking lot, dreaming about what you and Todd will do today and where you will do it, things get eerily still. Just before you open the door to Starbucks, you feel the barometric pressure drop, which causes you to look up. Low and behold, that distant thunderhead is now right on top of you and is a black wall of voodoo that's got the finger of God, a death-dealing, F-4 twister coming out of the wall cloud. Immediately you grab the door to try to get in and find some structure to hide behind, but you're too late. The tornado sucks you into a natural disaster, you're transported to Oz, surrounded by flying devil monkeys, and you're now conversing with a cowardly tin man.

That's why I hate tornados.

I have enough unexpected bunkum going on without having the violent vortex variable added to *mi vida*.

Hurricanes, though wickedly devastating, give you about a month to get the hizzle out of the way. If you die in a hurricane, you're stupid. Or you're deaf, blind, and don't have any friends. The NOAA dudes over-warn us during the hurricane's approach, for God's sake. They don't just show up like a tornado. They waddle across the Atlantic like Courtney Love bumping across a nightclub dance floor after seven *Cuervo* shots. The weather boys now are pretty spot on as to where the 'cane is going to make landfall. Tornados on the other hand drop out of the sky like Jason Voorhees, flinging cows, wielding a machete, and making you run through sheet rock.

According to Jesus' first sermon, when He shot across the bow of us booger-picking mortals, He promised both the good and bad, those who "built well," and those who built a rat trap, the holy and the profane, Mother Theresa and Sista Souljah, one and all, will get slammed-danced in this life.

That's both crews. The goodies and the baddies.

Not just the evil weeds.

All of us.

He formally forewarned everybody sucking air to brace for life's crunch.

Rains …

Floods …

Winds …

… will burst against our "house."

I wonder what "burst" means in the Greek? I'm guessin' it solidly falls into the bad crap category.

Why Would a Good God Allow
Bad Things to Happen to Good People?

No doubt, some of you are thinking, "Why *would* a good God allow bad things to happen to good people?" Good people? I don't know who these good people are. I keep bumping into sinners down here in Miami. Maybe I need to move to Mayberry, RFD.

I've got a question for those that table the good people stuff: good, compared to whom? Howard Stern? Katy Perry? Kid Rock? Jenna Jameson? I was watching an *E! True Hollywood* story the other day about Jameson and she was saying how she believes she will go to Heaven when she dies because she is a good person. She cares for her friends, she loves animals, and somehow those two ditties negate her need for Christ's redeeming sacrifice and offset all the familial heartache, cultural filth, STDs, drug abuse, masturbation, fornication, adultery, lesbianism, rape, and murder her porn videos have spawned within our society. If I were you, Jenna, I'd cease and desist the "I'm a good porn girl" garbage and just ask Christ to have mercy on your mucked up life.

C'mon, folks. Can't we drop the "I'm a good person stuff," like right now? Because according to the Bible, we're all turds, or more properly put, lost, wrapped in sin, and covered with rebellious sauce. And if we got what we deserved we would not be happy, Clappy.

There's nobody living right, not even one, nobody who knows the score, nobody alert for God. They've all taken the wrong turn; they've all wandered down blind alleys. No one's living right; I can't find a single one. Their throats are open graves, their tongues slick as mud slides. Every word they speak is tinged with poison. They open their mouths and pollute the air. They race for the honor of sinner-of-the-year, litter the land with heartbreak and ruin, don't know the first thing about living with others. They never give God the time of day ... we've compiled this long and sorry record as sinners (both us and them) and proved that we are utterly incapable of living the glorious lives God wills for us ... (Romans 3:10-18; 23, MSG)

Here's an acid test for those still not convinced that they're "all that bad" and thus don't "deserve" a storm. Allow my buddy, Slappy White, to wiretap your phone, record all private conversations and text messages, and video all your actions for the next year. Then, after the year of twenty-four/ seven surveillance, Slappy will take all of your less-than-shiny moments and put them on YouTube for the whole globe to take a gander. I'm not a gambling man, but if I were, after that video goes online, I'd be willing to wager that you wouldn't be talking the "I'm a good person" smack any longer.

In addition to dropping that "I'm a good guy" spiel, I will also venture to say that after all your buddies, family members, and work mates get to see your antics you'll also soon become friendless, cut out of your family's will, and jobless. Your only *friend* quite possibly could be an online, sexy eighteen-year-old girl named Brandi from L.A. who's really an obese, balding fifty-four-year old propane dealer named Cletus who lives in Light-a-Fart, USA. Yep, I think you'll drop that Betty Crocker rhetoric faster than Osama Bin Laden would a pickled pig's foot served by a pirate hooker if we could simply film that thing you call a life and play it for the planet.

The Problem of Pain

Why is pain a part of the human experience? I'm blaming Satan and Rosie O'Donnell. Other than those twins being culpable for human suffering, why God allows what He does, I don't fully know. Heck, I can't even figure out women or homosexuals; how am I supposed to know what's going on in His divine noggin'?

If you've got the time to wade into such weighty topics, go ahead; knock yourself out. I will gladly let all you heavy thinking wizards wrap your brain around its axle with philosophic inquiries into the quandary of human suffering in relation to God's omnipotence and His benevolence. Go for it.

Anyway, I'm too hectic, too finite, and too funky to figure out the Infinite One's transrational and incomprehensible mysterious ways. That stuff is above my pay grade, as Obama would say. So ... good luck. I've got two kids to put through college, geez Louise. I'm trying to figure out how to do that.

FYI: C.S. Lewis already answered the inquiry into pain and suffering in his atheist-slamming tome, *The Problem of Pain*.

So, little ol' redneck me will simply take the Son of God's word for it that storms are coming. We're all gonna go through hell, so I'm trying to prep for it as well as a goofy, Spirit-led sinner can when it comes knocking on my door because Jesus told us it is not a matter of *if* storms will come, but *when* storms will come.

To be forewarned is forearmed, eh?

So, let's just dispense with the, "I'm good and I don't deserve storms," blather. If we got what we deserved for what we have said and done, to both God and men, we'd be in the crunchy bucket at KFC. I personally cannot believe that I haven't gone, and don't continue to go, through major tsunamis every day for my past, present, and future sinfulness. The only thing I merit is a front row seat on the eighth concentric circle of Dante's *Inferno*. Yes, I wonder why a good God would allow *good* things to happen to a bad Doug.

What we do know about why God allows storms to come is gathered in the pronouncement of their pending presence— they are foundation testers. Storms, plain and simple, are provers of the substance of our subsistence.

They're just a test.

Like all tests, if we have done our due diligence we'll be okay.

I remember when I went to work for Sam's Club back in college. If we made it through the initial interviewing process we had to undergo one last screening, namely, the pee in the Dixie cup drug test. Since I hadn't been doing blow or bong hits for quite some time, I sailed through with flying colors. My dope smokin' buddy we nicknamed Awood, was not so lucky on his urination examination. His pee was loaded down with more THC than Snoop Dogg's entire fleet of bongs. Poor Awood.

I view storms as life's midterms, presented to make us fit for our final exam. Of course, this final assessment is a little graver than it would be, say, for one's English Lit course. If we fail Heaven's final we will not *get* an F. We will *be* F'd—meaning forsaken, of course. And we cannot retake the course.

Yep, storms tell on us.

They reveal how we have built our lives.

If we have built our existence on His Word, He said we'd ride the storm out. However, if we have been bull-headed and have built it on our own BS (belief systems) or have taken our cue from cultural crud, the storms will be a reality blast to a life ill founded.

Let me ask you a question.

Would you think I was a moron if I bought a double wide trailer house, put its skids on a stack of cinderblocks right on a South Florida beach, and then expected that barely anchored, flimsy structure to survive a Cat 5 hurricane?

Short answer—duh.

In addition, would I sound goofy if, after a wicked storm obliterated my feeble, beach-based bungalow and I was wedged thirty feet up in a palm tree with a coconut stuck up my backside, I told the weather chick from *Channel 7 News* who was reporting on the aftermath of the storm that I didn't know why God would allow this to happen to me?

Why would God allow this to happen to me, indeed?

Hey, someone get a stupid sticker and put it on my forehead. Get a pellet gun and shoot me.

Why did *God?!*

I'll tell me why. I'm an idiot. I built a hurricane magnet in hurricane central. I blew off wisdom, building codes, common sense, and erected a house of cards in a hurricane corridor. Had I built to post-hurricane Andrew stringent standards, there would have been a fair–to–middlin' chance that my house would have made it through a brutal storm with only a few downed trees and assorted debris.

But no. I built crap, and crap happened.

Pause and meditate.

In summation, little kiddies, what is the first impression Jesus put to us critters in Matthew's account of His initial major address? Expect storms. I said, He said, we should … expect storms. We should live in light of having, at times, the snot kicked out of us spiritually, physically, nationally, financially, emotionally, relationally, etc., and blah, blah, blah.

What else did He brand us with?

Build well.

Don't put a trailer house on the beach and expect it to endure 150 mph winds and a twenty-foot storm surge. In lieu of all of us being in line for some sort of storm, Jesus exhorts us to build well, and even though He won't exempt us from garbage, He told us we will survive, even thrive, when the poop hits the fan—if, *if*, we build our lives on the principles of His Word.

Storms are coming.

That was one of the first things out of His mouth during His earthly ministry.

That's what He impressed upon His disciples.

His message hasn't changed.

Are we ready?

Chapter Two

Are You Gonna Cowboy Up or Lay There and Bleed?

Try to exclude the possibility of suffering which the order of nature and the existence of free wills involve, and you find that you have excluded life itself. —C.S. Lewis

Act like men. (1 Corinthians 16:13, NASB)

Since pain is a given for us goobers, we have got to toughen up a bit and stop blathering about every little thing that pinches our tender pink flesh.

Especially, you guys.

When you complain, sir, you sound oh, so (how can I put this nicely?) ... lame.

As a man who is a Christian and was born and raised in Texas, as far as I'm concerned, according to the holy text, my Texas roots, and the testosterone fog in which I dwell, you are formally disallowed to whine. The only whine you're allowed to have is the one without the "h" that comes in a box and you drink with your steak.

Got that, girlie-man?

Um, you do know that God sent a whole stack of belly aching, low pain tolerant, Old Testament toads to an early roast in hell because they grumbled too much, don't cha? You don't? Yeah, He did. Check it out here …

> *And don't grumble as some of them did, for that is why God sent his angel of death to destroy them. All these events happened to them as examples for us. They were written down to warn us, who live at the time when this age is drawing to a close.* (1 Corinthians 10:10-11, NLT)

Thank God, He doesn't still doesn't punish whiners that harshly anymore!

Or does He?

Hmmm …

If we're going to thrive in life we have got to have a high pain tolerance and a rock-n-rolla attitude.

Jesus told us pressure is a piece of the pie of life in a jacked-up world. He impressed that upon us the first major time He opened His *boca*. He went through the meat grinder. Do we think we're better than Him? Answer … no.

God's sinless Son suffered. As dorky freaks in a mucked-up world, we'd better believe pain is going to be part and parcel of the days of our lives. Therefore, we've got to become cowboys who can take a frickin' lickin' and keep on tickin' and not be the squeally little puss-n-boots who bleats when the kitchen heats.

Can you dig it?

Shameless Plug Alert! I wrote the book on having the bulldog attitude. Do yourself, God, your family, and nation a favor and log on to Amazon.com, click your mouse, melt your plastic, and purchase my hot little read entitled: *The Bulldog Attitude: Get it or Get Left Behind.* Get five extra copies for your friends who tend to cry a little too much.

Having a tough hide is a jagged little pill to swallow seeing that our country has, of late, become officially wussified. We've turned into one big nation of squishy, blame-shifting, passive, OMG's, that if anything at anytime ruffles our feathers, disallows us to text message, forbids us to log on to Facebook, get a boob job, botox injections, lip implants, or buy Jimmy Choo shoes, we run screaming to the psychiatrist's couch and spend the next ten years taking up his time and sucking down doc's prescription meds.

And that's just the guys!

Our churches and the Christians who fill them are not any better. I was going to say *much* instead of *any*. But I'd be lying to myself. We are way, way up on the wussy graph as far as our collective goes. Yep, we're spiking the Wuss-O-Meter.

Which is weird?

Why is it weird?

Well, you'd think that Christians would be the very ones who would be able to take whatever hell throws at us, principally because we are tied, supposedly, to the One who defeated death, hell, and the grave. You'd think that we would be a tad pluckier, wouldn't you? If you would, you be dead on, because we should.

Scripture states that the biblical Christian is to be an overcomer. In our vernacular that would be a buttkicker.

Do you think anyone is going to be able to drive a wedge between us and Christ's love for us? There is no way! Not trouble, not hard times, not hatred, not hunger, not homelessness, not bullying threats, not backstabbing, not even the worst sins listed in Scripture: "They kill us in cold blood because they hate you. We're sitting ducks; they pick us off one by one." None of this fazes us because Jesus loves us. I'm absolutely convinced that nothing—nothing living or dead, angelic or demonic, today or tomorrow, high or low, thinkable or unthinkable—absolutely nothing can get between us and God's love because of the way that Jesus our Master has embraced us. (Romans 8:35-39, MSG)

Happy in all things—operative word *all* ...

> Celebrate God all day, every day. I mean, revel in him ... I've learned by now to be quite content whatever my circumstances. I'm just as happy with little as with much, with much as with little. I've found the recipe for being happy whether full or hungry, hands full or hands empty. Whatever I have, wherever I am, I can make it through anything in the One who makes me who I am. (Philippians 4: 4; 11b-13, MSG)

We understand that even bad crap strangely works out in our favor ...

> Meanwhile, the moment we get tired in the waiting, God's Spirit is right alongside helping us along. If we don't know how or what to pray, it doesn't matter. He does our praying in and for us, making prayer out of our wordless sighs, our aching groans. He knows us far better than we know ourselves, knows our pregnant condition, and keeps us present before God. That's why we can be so sure that every detail in our lives of love for God is worked into something good. (Romans 8:26-28, MSG)

That even when men do evil to us, it's cool because God strangely works it out for good.

"But as for you, ye thought evil against me; but God meant it unto good ... " (Genesis 50:20, KJV).

But not us. We weep like a twelve-year-old little chick when we don't get our way, when life doesn't kiss us on the cheek, or God doesn't make us rich by Saturday. The great men and women of the Bible weren't like this generation of pusillanimous Christians, who are oh, so limp and lame.

For example, check out this laundry list of yuckiness that Paul had to schlep through, and pay particular attention to his attitude when dealing with serious poo-poo. I'm talkin' crapo *el grande*.

> *In everything we do we try to show that we are true ministers of God. We patiently endure troubles and hardships and calamities of every kind. We have been beaten, been put in jail, faced angry mobs, worked to exhaustion, endured sleepless nights, and gone without food. We have proved ourselves by our purity, our understanding, our patience, our kindness, our sincere love, and the power of the Holy Spirit. We have faithfully preached the truth. God's power has been working in us. We have righteousness as our weapon, both to attack and to defend ourselves. We serve God whether people honor us or despise us, whether they slander us or praise us. We are honest, but they call us impostors. We are well known, but we are treated as unknown. We live close to death, but here we are, still alive. We have been beaten within an inch of our lives. Our hearts ache, but we always have joy. We are poor, but we give spiritual riches to others. We own nothing, and yet we have everything.* (2 Corinthians 6:4-10, NLT)

From that rebuke check out what the boys and girls in the Hall of Faith of Hebrews 11 had to plow through:

> *Well, how much more do I need to say? It would take too long to recount the stories of the faith of Gideon, Barak, Samson, Jephthah, David, Samuel, and all the prophets. By faith these people overthrew kingdoms,*

ruled with justice, and received what God had promised them. They shut the mouths of lions, quenched the flames of fire, and escaped death by the edge of the sword. Their weakness was turned to strength. They became strong in battle and put whole armies to flight. Women received their loved ones back again from death. But others trusted God and were tortured, preferring to die rather than turn from God and be free. They placed their hope in the resurrection to a better life. Some were mocked, and their backs were cut open with whips. Others were chained in dungeons. Some died by stoning, and some were sawed in half; others were killed with the sword. Some went about in skins of sheep and goats, hungry and oppressed and mistreated. They were too good for this world. They wandered over deserts and mountains, hiding in caves and holes in the ground. All of these people we have mentioned received God's approval because of their faith, yet none of them received all that God had promised. For God had far better things in mind for us that would also benefit them, for they can't receive the prize at the end of the race until we finish the race. (Hebrews 11:32-40, NLT)

Not only did they go through external excrement from friends and foes with a winning attitude, they also dealt with the self-inflicted pain of personal failure without renouncing God, getting a nose ring, and quitting life. For instance, check out these private *faux pas* by the Hebrew's 11 crew, which caused them personal pain aplenty:

Abraham: Old Abe had sex with his maid Hagar. Oops. Rule number one, ladies: if you're looking to employ a girl to work in your house and around your husband, never hire a maid that has more than three teeth. Also, make sure your housekeeper has a lazy eye, gorilla arms, smells like pickles and cigarettes, and has an IQ of fifty so that "Abraham" won't be tempted to shag her to fulfill the promise of God.

The thing that blows my mind about the Abraham/Hagar thing is that Sarah, his wife, is the one who suggested that Abraham bump uglies with Hagar. I know one thing for certain. Abraham's wife was not Italian. Another interesting ditty about Abe's dalliance was when his wife suggested that he and Hagar get together, he didn't say no. He didn't rebuke her. He didn't hesitate. That's some wacky stuff right there, folks.

Noah: After Jehovah gave the planet a forty day crash course on why it is important to know how to swim if you're going to blow off His commandments, Noah got so wasted that he passed out drunk on the ground naked.

Moses: Mo started his ministry not by feeding the poor, not by setting up a prophetic website, a Twitter and Facebook page with a PayPal link, not by begging Paul and Jan Crouch to let him sing his new song, "I Was a Baby in a Basket Because Pharaoh Blew a Gasket." Nope, Moses started his ministry off by murdering an Egyptian and burying his body in his backyard. Moses was acting more like George Costanza than Christ Jesus. Holy homicide, Batman!

Samson: Samson was a great judge in saving Israel from its enemies, but a horrible judge when it came to picking chicks to date. Evidently, Samson didn't dig the girls in his church's singles group and decided to go fishing in the pagan pond for a lady and took a shining to a devil-woman named Delilah. That ended up costing him his commitment to God, his coif, his eyeballs, and caused his early brutal death by being crushed by giant stone pillars. Other than that, things went pretty well for Sam.

David: David, a man after God's own heart, kinda lost his bearings one day and whooped it up with his neighbor's wife and then had her husband murdered. Hello! Wow, Davey. The wheels sort of came off your car there, man. What happened? Why didn't you try golfing or something or … get a Corvette?

When I get to Heaven, I want to ask Bathsheba what the heck was she thinking when she decided to take a bath on the roof of her condo in full view of David. Witchy woman.

Interestingly enough, you don't see Abraham, Noah, Moses, Samson, or David get on *Oprah*, lie to Geraldo, file lawsuits against McDonald's, make excuses, bee-bop, explain away, manipulate, or mitigate the fallout and the pain from their personal BS. Rather, by grace they rode out the storm they had created 'til it petered out on the beach.

And what about Jesus on the Cross? He cowboyed through the Cross and those three days in hell without acting like a whiny Christian.

> *Keep your eyes on Jesus, who both began and finished this race we're in. Study how he did it. Because he never lost sight of where he was headed—that exhilarating finish in and with God— he could put up with anything along the way: cross, shame, whatever. And now he's there, in the place of honor, right alongside God. When you find yourselves flagging in your faith, go over that story again, item by item, that long litany of hostility he plowed through. That will shoot adrenaline into your souls! In this all-out match against sin, others have suffered far worse than you, to say nothing of what Jesus went through—all that bloodshed! So don't feel sorry for yourselves ...* (Hebrews 12:2-5a, MSG)

Talk about p-p-p-pain ... check out what happened to Jesus' original hombres/disciples. They had, uh, kind of a rough life. The following is from *Foxe's Book of Martyrs* ... in his words, not mine.

Stephen

St. Stephen suffered the next in order [after Jesus' crucifixion]. His death was occasioned by the faithful manner in which he preached the Gospel to the betrayers and murderers of Christ. To such a degree of madness were they excited, that they cast him out of the city and stoned him to death.

James the Great

The next martyr we meet with, according to St. Luke, in the History of the Apsotles' Acts, was James the son of Zebedee, the elder brother of John, and a relative of our Lord; for his mother Salome was cousin-german to the Virgin Mary. It was not until ten years after the death of Stephen that the second martyrdom took place; for no sooner had Herod Agrippa been appointed governor of Judea, than, with a view to ingratiate himself with them, he raised a sharp persecution against the Christians, and determined to make an effectual blow, by striking at their leaders. The account given us by an eminent primitive writer, Clemens Alexandrinus, ought not to be overlooked; that, as James was led to the place of martyrdom, his accuser was brought to repent of his conduct by the apostle's extraordinary courage and undauntedness, and fell down at his feet to request his pardon, professing himself a Christian, and resolving that James should not receive the crown of martyrdom alone. Hence they were both beheaded at the same time.

Philip

Was born at Bethsaida, in Galilee and was first called by the name of "disciple." He labored diligently in Upper Asia, and suffered martyrdom at Heliopolis, in Phrygia. He was scourged, thrown into prison, and afterwards crucified, A.D. 54.

Matthew

Whose occupation was that of a toll-gatherer, was born at Nazareth. He wrote his gospel in Hebrew, which was afterwards translated into Greek by James the Less. The scene of his labors was Parthia, and Ethiopia, in which latter country he suffered martyrdom, being slain with a halberd in the city of Nadabah, A.D. 60.

James the Less

Is supposed by some to have been the brother of our Lord, by a former wife of Joseph. This is very doubtful, and accords too much with the Catholic superstition, that Mary never had any other children except our Savior. He was elected to the oversight of the churches of Jerusalem; and was the author of the Epistle ascribed to James in the sacred canon. At the age of ninety-four he was beaten and stoned by the Jews; and finally had his brains dashed out with a fuller's club.

Matthias

Of whom less is known than of most of the other disciples, was elected to fill the vacant place of Judas. He was stoned at Jerusalem and then beheaded.

Andrew

Was the brother of Peter. He preached the gospel to many Asiatic nations; but on his arrival at Edessa he was taken and crucified on a cross, the two ends of which were fixed transversely in the ground. Hence the derivation of the term, St. Andrew's Cross.

Mark

Was born of Jewish parents of the tribe of Levi. He is supposed to have been converted to Christianity by Peter, whom he served as an amanuensis, and under whose inspection he wrote his gospel in the Greek language. Mark was dragged to pieces by the people of Alexandria, at the great solemnity of Serapis their idol, ending his life under their merciless hands.

Peter

Among many other saints, the blessed apostle Peter was condemned to death, and crucified, as some do write, at Rome; albeit some others, and not without cause, do doubt thereof. Hegesippus saith that Nero sought matter against Peter to put him to death; which, when the people perceived, they entreated Peter with much ado that he would fly the city. Peter, through their importunity at length persuaded, prepared himself to avoid. But, coming to the gate, he saw the Lord Christ come to meet him, to whom he, worshipping, said, "Lord, whither dost Thou go?" To whom He answered and said, "I am come again to be crucified." By this, Peter, perceiving his suffering to be understood, returned into the city. Jerome saith that he was crucified, his head being down and his feet upward, himself so requiring, because he was (he said) unworthy to be crucified after the same form and manner as the Lord was.

Paul

Paul, the apostle, who before was called Saul, after his great travail and unspeakable labors in promoting the Gospel of Christ, suffered also in this first persecution under Nero. Abdias, declareth that under his execution Nero sent two of his esquires, Ferega and Parthemius, to bring him word of his death. They, coming to Paul instructing the people, desired him to pray for them, that they might believe; who told them that shortly after they should believe and be baptised at His sepulcher. This done, the soldiers came and led him out of the city to the place of execution, where he, after his prayers made, gave his neck to the sword.

Jude

The brother of James, was commonly called Thaddeus. He was crucified at Edessa, A.D. 72.

Bartholomew

Preached in several countries, and having translated the Gospel of Matthew into the language of India, he propagated it in that country. He was at length cruelly beaten and then crucified by the impatient idolaters.

Thomas

Called Didymus, preached the Gospel in Parthia and India, where exciting the rage of the pagan priests, he was martyred by being thrust through with a spear.

Luke

The evangelist, was the author of the Gospel which goes under his name. He travelled with Paul through various countries, and is supposed to have been hanged on an olive tree, by the idolatrous priests of Greece.

Simon

Surnamed Zelotes, preached the Gospel in Mauritania, Africa, and even in Britain, in which latter country he was crucified, A.D. 74.

John

The "beloved disciple," was brother to James the Great. The churches of Smyrna, Pergamos, Sardis, Philadelphia, Laodicea, and Thyatira, were founded by him. From Ephesus he was ordered to be sent to Rome, where it is affirmed he was cast into a cauldron of boiling oil. He escaped by miracle, without injury. Domitian afterwards banished him to the Isle of Patmos, where he wrote the Book of Revelation. Nerva, the successor of Domitian, recalled him. He was the only apostle who escaped a violent death.

Barnabas

Was of Cyprus, but of Jewish descent, his death is supposed to have taken place about A.D. 73.

And yet, notwithstanding all these continual persecutions and horrible punishments, the Church daily increased, deeply rooted in the doctrine of the apostles and watered plentously with the blood of saints.

Wow!

Now, compare the above heroes of the faith to the little nancy boy in your church's singles group who's crying over being deleted from the Facebook friends list of the girl he's been stalking. Yeah, freak perv boy is making the girl's legit rejection of him into a five-alarm fire and the reason why he now believes God does not exist.

What a helix-missing moron.

What an oxygen thief.

That guy should leave the Christian church and become a Satanist and go and screw up that demon-ogling, moronic assembly and quit fouling up Christ's Church.

Insane.

Excuse Me, But I Seem to Have Lost My Testicles

Y'know, back in the day, like in the days of Moses, if you were an Israelite man and you wanted to be one of Jehovah's warriors or possibly a priest, and you wanted a chunk of the Promised Land, God required you to have testicles. I ain't lying. See for yourself in Leviticus 21:20 and Deuteronomy

23:1-4. I'll bet you have never ever heard those two passages preached on before, have you?

Why would God require *His* boys have *their* boys intact? Why the testicular standard and fascination in the Old Covenant? Moreover, what spiritual significance does it have for Christians in New Testament times? Well, I'm glad you asked.

Testicles produce the male sex hormone testosterone, which promotes the development of the genital glands and the male secondary sexual characteristics, as well as having an influence on the overall growth and vigor of a dude.

Two of the manifest traits that come via the maturation of the *cojones* are, number one, the desire to breed, and number two, the desire to fight. These two traits make up two-thirds of God's original mandate for man in the Book of Genesis.

Biologically speaking, without the testicles the drive to fight and the desire to multiply vanish like the Constitution at an ACLU rally. Need an example? Let's go to creation and look at the animal kingdom. Think about it. A stallion is a wild and hard-to-handle horse. And his neutered counterpart, the gelding, well … he is a twenty-first-century Christian—submissive and easy. A bull is notably wilder than his castrated counterpart the ox, which is a lethargic grass-muncher just waiting around to become stew meat.

You know, it's a compliment, at least I think it is, to be called a stallion or to be bullish. In the natural realm the *cojones* produce confidence, comedy, courage, and competition, among other things. And given the natural characteristics that these mature *tomatoes* produce and how they typify the corresponding spiritual equivalent of having guts or courage, it's easy to see why Satan would seek to spiritually neuter and create an ecclesiastical impotency among the men and women who make up the Church of the living God. And you know what? Satan has done a darn good job of spiritually castrating the Body of Christ. Many of us have lost our holy tenacity, the ability to fight, the capacity to take pain, and the propensity to cowboy up.

The Church used to be known for brave missionaries, shakers and shapers of societies, rock-n-rollas who might weeble and wobble, but they wouldn't stay down. For millennia, Christ's Church spawned bold prophets and apostles who, by God's grace, could weather any storm and come out smelling like Febreze.

Not now.

And here's the reason why: we've gotten rid of prophets and have replaced them with politically correct, nutless wonder puppets, and have driven off the men and their masculine trait of taking pain in stride.

Allow me to illustrate ...

Wussies Beget Wussies

Can you imagine Clint Eastwood coming to one of our highly feminized evangelical churches? Yeah, Dirty Harry himself pulls up in the parking lot in his black Range Rover amidst the sea of mini-vans, station wagons, and pink Miatas.

Picture it. See Eastwood ascending the steps to the church entrance where he's greeted by four women and one man. The too-excited, quasi-male greeter hands Clint a pastel-colored flyer covering all the weddings, baby showers, birthdays, and picnics.

Moving past these greeters, Clint is then hit with more contrived hugs than at a Richard Simmons support group. Attempting to avoid this barrage of groping, flabby arms from people he does not know, but now is immediately expected to hug, he tries to fade from view and take refuge against the wall and out of the way. But the floral arrangements are so profuse it makes an FTD warehouse look like the Mojave Desert.

Finally out of reach and trying hard to avoid eye contact with anyone, Clint keeps his gaze on the artwork. On his right are six matching prints of fat baby angels in Little Rascal poses, looking like they have a good buzz going from their mommy's milk that's been liberally laced with Vicodin. On his left are three other pieces of artwork that depict Jesus, Peter, and John the Baptist all in aggravated states of angst looking more like the Victorian view of a woman rather than heralds of the greatest story ever told.

Finally, it's go time.

Clint strides into the pink and teal sanctuary, taking his seat amidst a crowd that's made up of 80 percent women, 1 percent masculine men, and 19 percent quasi-males.

The music begins.

It's aphoristic and cliché riddled. It's subjective, reflective, emotional, and a bit erotic, talking about Jesus being my lover. After the song leader finishes the "worship," he then commands the congregation to turn around and … here it goes again … "Hug three people and tell them you love them with the love of the Lord."

At which time, Eastwood makes his exit, not being able to take this effeminate crap any longer.

Consciously or unconsciously, Clint realizes that to convert to this brand of Christianity he must sacrifice not only his sins, but also his God-given, innate, masculine traits that Jehovah naturally hard-wired him with.

This ain't the stuff of greatness.

This is gooeyness.

This is us. And this is why we wash out when we start to go through hell. An effeminate environment has made us a bunch of Oscar Mayer weenies.

Weak leaders produce weak people.

Wussy environments spawn wussies.

If we wanna have a high pain tolerance to ride out the storms, then we must bring men and masculinity back into the house of God. Period.

But men who would be men aren't beating a path to get into the postmodern pews.

Shameless Plug Alert! You must, must, get my audio book *God's Warriors & Wild Men: Why Men Hate Church and What to do About It.* This CD or audio download slam dances the lame effete funk that has wrecked the Body of Christ. I expose the roots and the fruits of our rank effeminacy and table the antidote for our squeamish girlie-man malaise. Go to ClashRadio.com and buy it now!

We now return to my incredible, entertaining, and incisive book.

Dude Looks Like a Lady

Have you ever asked yourself, "Self, why do churches today look more like the bra and panty department at Wal-Mart, rather than a battalion of saints poised to whup some demonic backside?"

Why do men avoid going to church, and what can be done about it?

Here's the veneer-stripped-away answer: Church, for most men, has not only become irrelevant, it has also become effeminate and most men, more than anything, want to be masculine.

The current lack of strong men within the Church, both in the numeric and leadership sense, has crippled our cathedrals and has helped devastate our nation ethically.

So how do we regain the masculine spirit in our houses of worship?

1. Put an end to preaching by nancy boys, right *now!* It freaks us meat eaters out. Get it? Hire a pastor who throws off a good John Wayne vibe instead of that Boy George feeling.

2. Ditto regarding the worship/music leader. And make sure your new testosterone-laden *songmeister* is outfitted with weighty worship music instead of saccharine-laced slush.

3. Enough with the *Precious Moments* prints and figurines, okay? How about decking out the sanctuary with serious transcendent artwork that stops us in our tracks, rather than ubiquitous prints of fat baby angels who look like they've got a good buzz going from too much Mountain Dew and children's aspirin?

4. Lose the Church's "I'm in therapy forever" feel. Yes, yes, we're all "a work in progress," but the co-dependant, extended womb the Church has wrongfully created has prevented congregants from getting a life because of some difficult crap they've been dealt.

If the Church wants to recover its losses, toughen up a tad. We've got to draw the knuckle draggers back to church.

Masculine men are pretty easy.

Toss in reason, competition, initiation, struggle, fun, a problem to spiritually throttle, and we'll be there like stink on a monkey. Blow off, suppress, and spiritually emasculate the environment of these holy testicular necessities and your church, as far as men go, will be emptier than Mary Kate's and Ashley's stomachs.

We need men who teach the congregation, especially the guys, to leave mommy's familiar, safe haven and venture out into the danger zone, to find their Holy Grail.

- To say hello to the strange.
- To welcome the unfamiliar.
- To protect people, lead people, rescue people.
- To fight inequities and absurdities.
- To beware of parents and pastors who want to "mother" you.
- To avoid the secure, fear over-protection, and happily accept the masculine task of the holy cowboy.
- To get to a place where pain is not a big deal; where you embrace the battle.
- To cowboy up instead of lay there and bleed.

- And to be an example of ballsiness that will encourage others to resist self-doubt, squeamishness, indecision, and the impulse to surrender and withdraw into the warm, wet womb of Wussville.

So you wanna be a cowboy, baby?

I hope so, because if not, I don't think you're gonna make it through what life is about to toss you.

Chapter Three

It's About Character, Stupid

PERFECT GOODNESS CAN NEVER DEBATE ABOUT THE END
TO BE ATTAINED, AND PERFECT WISDOM CANNOT DEBATE
ABOUT THE MEANS MOST SUITED TO ACHIEVE IT.

—C.S. LEWIS

When a person is "born again," there will be an extreme makeover in said person's life changing them from being a dilatory dillweed to a dynamic person. Yep, when God, the Holy Spirit, moves into our trailer house, there will be radical transformation.

Can you say, "R-A-D-I-C-A-L?"

I knew you could.

As soon as Christ's blood is applied to our sin-laden soul's account, God kicks us out of the driver's seat. It's move over, Rover ... God's taking over. He's not going to let us stay in charge and do whatever the heck we wanna do. We're His now. Can you dig it? We are not going to stay the same. Jesus has a jackhammer that He loves and He isn't afraid to use it on us. As Van Halen once sang, we will experience massive c-c-change. Nuthin' stays the same.

For instance, if you're a mean, ugly, sad, and bitter devil-woman, Jesus is going to jack with you until you become sweet, pleasant, happy, and a forgiving angel-babe who people like to hang around instead of pouring gasoline on and kicking into an open campfire.

Need another illustration?

Let's say you're a tenth-degree horndog, a forty-one-year-old male who still lives with mommy, whose brutally stupid carnal core revels in the dictates of your dictates. Guess what? Jesus is going to go medieval on you to eradicate those repulsive roots.

Now for those who hate their personal crud, the above is music to your ears because God's presence means liberation from the smack that has been a royal pain in your butt for the last umpteen years.

Hallelujah!

This makes me happy.

Matter of fact, I think I'll celebrate in homage to Christ's liberating clout in my cruddy life. Back in a minute …

All right, where were we?

Oh yeah, transformation.

As stated, when God takes up residence in our lives He immediately starts remodeling our thinking according to what He likey. And you know what He likey? He likey His Son and … and … He wants His blood bought boys and girls to reflect the character of Christ and not their wacky aunt with the mustache. Or as Paul put it …

> *God knew what he was doing from the very beginning. He decided from the outset to shape the lives of those who love him along the same lines as the life of his Son. The Son stands first in the line of humanity he restored. We see the original and intended shape of our lives there in him. After God made that decision of what his children should be like, he followed it up by*

calling people by name. After he called them by name, he set them on a solid basis with himself. And then, after getting them established, he stayed with them to the end, gloriously completing what he had begun. (Romans 8:29-30, MSG)

It's not easy, even for God, to transform our hearts and souls to reflect His attitudes and actions. It's going to be rough, folks, as our natural bent is toward selfishness, and Jesus' is toward selflessly pleasing the Father. To get us into that frame of mind will take a crowbar and some C4 because we do not naturally float in that altruistic direction. At least I don't.

I'm sure being Christ-like is easy for some of you angels, but not for *moi*. I find my heart twisted, my soul black, my mind mendicant, and my spirit just plain weird. God has to Gitmo me to step and fetch in His direction, and Gitmo me He will. Let the waterboarding begin!

According to Jeremiah, our hearts are deceitfully wicked and desperately sick, which begs him to ask the question—who can truly know how creepy it is? (See Jeremiah 17:9.) The gospel declares that only, I mean only, Jesus via the Holy Spirit, can enact such a heart change. No amount of Tony Robbins' CDs, Deepak Chopra seminars, New Year's resolutions, Yanni music, candle lighting, or going to the gym is going to change a heart that, according to the Scripture, is darker than Snoop Dogg's bong stem.

Nothing and no one.

Christ alone.

Not Buddha. Sure as heck, not Mohammed. Not Danny Partridge. Only Christ.

Sola Scriptura, Sola Fide, Sola Gratia, Solus Christus, Soli Deo Gloria. Amen and Amen. I think I'll have another cigar because I just made myself happy, and when Doug gets happy, it's time for a stogie. Come here, Camacho.

Yep, according to the sacred text, when one asks Christ into their SNAFU-ed life, the triune Godhead replaces our stony stubborn hearts with a heart that doesn't dig in its heels and demand its own way like a spoiled little metrosexual. Sorry for the slight, Seacrest. Rather, we get a new gravitational pull toward godliness and greatness, which replaces our former proclivities toward pukiness. (See 2 Corinthians 5:17.) Pukiness is a Latin word (*L. pukinirito*) which means all the crap you have said and done that you're not really looking forward to having everyone see at the Judgment Seat. Hello.

I liken the process and the act of salvation to what a buddy of mine went through when he got married. The girl he betrothed had what the therapeutic community would call multiple personality disorder. An exorcist would call it a stack of devils. This chick was William Peter Blatty material to the tenth power.

We tried to warn him, but he was blinded by lust, I mean love, and since he was following the commands of his hormones, he forged on and married multiple Milly. Isn't it interesting how the "Holy Spirit" so often lines up with our lusts? Hmmm ... Of course the wedding was glorious, the champagne flowed, and the wedding night was crazy. However, soon after the nuptials Milly spawned enough *personas* to form their own soccer league and life began to get, let's say, hellish. His marriage turned to mayhem. We tried to warn him about her complexities, but when the blood flows from the head to the crotch, one becomes impervious to information and exhortation.

Can I get a witness, gentlemen?

Now before someone thinks I just blasphemed, I am not comparing Christ to some demon-possessed chick. I'm a unfinished person and that crude analogy I volleyed was to make the point that Christ is a multi-faceted Messiah, and to not know that when one says "Yes" to Him, or to believe that He is only a celestial sugar daddy in the sky, ready at your beck and call to give you whatever the heck you want, is to set oneself up to be rudely awakened by His other personas once the deal is sealed.

You see, American Christians believe that life with God should be nothing but birds chirping twenty-four/seven. The problem is that God has a pellet gun and He likes to shoot our birds.

It goes something like this: we want to go to Heaven, not because we're repentant but because we're selfish, and let's face it, who the heck wants to go to hell? We hate staying at a Holiday Inn, so hell is out of the question. Next, if you're a single dude, you want God to give you a wife that has the heart of Mother Theresa and the body of Kim Kardashian and a sex drive that is up there with a drunken alley cat's. After that, we'd like an Escalade and a six, no, seven figure job. No skip the job, just give us the money jackpot, Jesus. In addition, God, we'd appreciate no stress, no pain, no traffic jams, a body that stays fit without exercise, and no inflamed hemorrhoidal tissue. That's all.

Essentially, American Christians want God to be their personal Obama bailout deity who springs them free from every trap that they've gotten themselves into; a veritable Santa Christ here to give them everything that their lower cortex, monkey brain begs for.

Yes, we've come to expect such service. I'm sorry; we've come to *demand* such service. And for good reason. That's the pile of bollocks most preachers have told us dorky Americans to expect from the eternal one. The only problem is those earthly perks from our good God are only a small piece of the salvation pie. The rest of that pizza is all about us being hammered into what He desires, which 99.9 percent of the time conflicts with our desires. (I'm trying to be easy on you. It's actually 110 percent of the time.) Need a tissue?

The process of us being processed—or as Santo Pablo put it in Romans 8, "conformed" into the image of the Son—begins right after you say, "Please God, forgive me." After that salvific plea one usually begins to experience heavenly emotions. You *feel* the love of God. His presence is nearly tangible. The air is fresher, the wine is sweeter, your neighbors aren't such a pain in the butt, life is lovelier (traffic still sucks), but by in large, your life, in the gentle arms of God, is pretty sa-weet. It's like you're starring in a Hallmark commercial.

We love the sweet times, don't we? We never want them to end. Why? Well, when we pray, He answers. When we sing His praises, gold glitter falls from our ceiling, Gabriel the archangel shows up in your bedroom ready to be dispatched to get you a South Florida condo, and the smell of fresh cut roses mysteriously fills the air. Who would want that to end?

No one would, except God, of course.

The reason why?

Well, we're all selfish mooks and all those heavenly experiences usually do not change a person from being a liar, a cheat, a rebel toad, a porn freak, or a goober who's dumber than both Harry and Lloyd.

Since God has an agenda which includes you morphing into a quasi-likeness of Jesus and then becoming gifted and graced to be a player on this planet, sweet and cuddly honeymoon Jehovah turns off your Andrea Bocelli CD and turns into the drill sergeant in *Full Metal Jacket* and officially begins the process of kicking your spiritually saggy butt into shape. Attennnn-*tion!*

Welcome to "Hell School" where character is king and the Holy Spirit is a stubborn nun with a ruler.

A Gentleman? A Dove? A Lover? Or a Blow Torch?

I indeed baptize you with water unto repentance: but he that cometh after me is mightier than I, whose shoes I am not worthy to bear: he shall baptize you with the Holy Ghost, and with fire. (Matthew 3:11, KJV)

How many of you have heard the evangelical bunkum that the Holy Spirit is a gentleman and that when He wants to get your attention, He'll woo you like a lover? I know, kinda weird, eh?

Woo you like a lover? What is this? Liza Minnelli Christianity? No wonder men hate church. The fact that, as a man, I have actually heard that kind of analogy used to explain God in a church, shows you how effeminate evangelical ecclesia has become.

A Gentleman? A Wooer? A Lover? Put the massage oils down and walk away, Pastor Spanky.

What about this analogy regarding the Holy Spirit?

The Holy Spirit is like a dove, i.e., cooing and pretty … have you heard that one? The Holy Spirit is a pretty bird? Again, kind of a girlie comparison, eh? Y'know, the Holy Spirit descended like a dove one time and He's forever branded as a cooing bird by effete evangelical hosts. Great. If I were the Holy Spirit, I'd be ticked. A gentleman, wooer, lover, and now a dove? Just go ahead, icky evangelicals, and couch the Third Person of the Godhead as some celestial Liberace and drive off all the dudes from the Church, why don't you?

I like to kick it old school when referring to the Spirit of the Living God and refer to him as King Jimmy did as the Holy Ghost. He's holy and a ghost. That's more awe inspiring and more conducive to inducing fear into my soul, which keeps me more in line. (See Proverbs 1:7.) But that's just me—and Paul and Peter and Ezekiel and Jeremiah and David and John the Baptist. Wooing gentlemen and cooing doves don't really faze me. I hate mock civility and I hunt doves.

When John the Baptist, Heaven's emcee for Earth's main event, i.e., the baptism and earthly ministry of Jesus Christ, spoke of Jesus' ministry and the role of the Holy Spirit in one's life, he likened the Spirit's work to a baptism of fire. An immersion into an inferno. Not a cooing dove. Not a wafty wooer. Not a polite gentleman. But a flame, a kiln, a torch. A fire baptizer. Can you say, "Fire?"

Y'know the last time I checked, fire is hot. Like real hot. Like *muy caliente* hot. Like very uncomfortable if it touches you directly hot. Yep, from my experience fire burns, consumes, and permanently alters pretty much everything it comes in contact with.

For instance, if I were to handcuff my buddy Sling Blade's hand to a stair rail and then take out my oxygen acetylene torch and set his hand on fire for, oh … say, ten minutes, the character and nature of his hand would forever change, wouldn't you agree? Yeah … it would. I'm talkin' radical alteration. Suffice it to say that if he were a guitar player, he wouldn't be using that hand anymore to pick and play. If he were a chronic booger-picker, he'd have to use the other hand or his toes or chopsticks or something. The fire would fundamentally change how the fired appendage operated. Do you smell what I'm cooking?

When God the Holy Spirit begins to fire up our lives, it is for the purpose of purging our hearts from the impurities, compromises, proclivities, and unholy bents that lie deep within us, the saved sinners. A lot of fundamental, sweeping changes for the good in our lives come only through deep and drastic dealings with God in the inner man where we feel like we're going through hell, or as Peter called this phenomenon, a fiery ordeal, a strange thing.

> *Beloved, do not be surprised at the fiery ordeal among you, which comes upon you for your testing, as though some strange thing were happening to you.* (1 Peter 4:12, NASB)

Let Me Stand Next to Your Fire

Behold, I am going to send My messenger, and he will clear the way before Me. And the Lord, whom you seek, will suddenly come to His temple; and the messenger of the covenant, in whom you delight, behold, He is coming, says the LORD of hosts.

But who can endure the day of His coming? And who can stand when He appears? For He is like a refiner's fire and like fullers' soap.

And He will sit as a smelter and purifier of silver, and He will purify the sons of Levi and refine them like gold and silver, so that they may present to the LORD offerings in righteousness.

Then the offering of Judah and Jerusalem will be pleasing to the LORD as in the days of old and as in former years. (Malachi 3:1-4, NASB)

You gotta love the prophet's terse take on Christ in a day of rank political correctness, which extricates those aspects of Christ's character that are reprehensible to our soft *carne*. Malachi, the last of the Old Testament prophets (and the only Italian prophet), who foretold of Jesus' first coming, said the Son of God would come as a refiner's fire, to test and purify His people. That was the last revelation to the people of God regarding what they should expect when He officially entered into His earthly ministry.

A refiner?

Tests?

Soap?

Purification?

Screw that stuff.

And a smelter? A *smelter*?

Now when you think of the many names of Jesus, what we love to call Him, and how He's referred to in our churches by our pastors and our dainty worship leaders, have you ever, in your entire Christian experience, heard them talk about Jesus, the Smelter? We don't even know what a smelter is. Sounds like a Yiddish curse word for a slow driver. *Oy vey.*

Of all the analogies and the words at the disposal of the Holy Spirit (and you gotta know that His vocab is way more extensive than say, William Buckley's was), He chooses to refer to our sweet and cuddly, teddy bear Christ as a smelter. A smelter? Has the Holy Ghost gone nuts? To us, Jesus ain't no smelter. We don't even know what a smelter is and it sounds icky.

No, to the twenty-first century, soul strokin' narcissist who occupies the pew in our postmodern churches, He's a bike–riding, fluorescent-light-bulb-using environmentalist, or a motivational speaker with a curly mullet and a soft southern drawl. Or maybe He's a first century, spiritual Mr. Rogers with a light tan, Swedish blonde hair, and an Orlando Bloom-like scraggly, scraggly beard who would never, ever, purposefully put us into a raging fire as a real smelter would do to his metal ore. "Won't you be my neighbor?" Hello, neighbor.

We don't think of Jesus as a smelter, but the Trinity does, for what that's worth.

So what is a smelter? A smelter is someone who places the various metal ores into a raging flame in order to extract the metals they contain to fashion weapons, jewelry, or to use for currency. In other words, to get the gold, the ore's gotta burn.

To recap Malachi's analogy: in this drama, Jesus is the "smelter."

Guess who or what we are in this twisted theater? We are the "ore" with impurities. Impurities? Me? Like what? I'm a good person. Yeah, right. And I'm a fat, lesbian who voted for Obama and hates big-game hunting and sport fishing. Read Romans 1:18-32, 1 Corinthians 6:9-11, Ephesians 4:18-32, Galatians 5:19-21, and 2 Timothy 3:1-5 and try to tell me with a straight face that you don't have any impurities.

The "fire" in this production is life's intense internal and external sucky trials that we abhor and do not want to experience, but are necessary to purge the garbage out of our hearts. Yuck. That doesn't sound like fun. And you know what? It isn't joyful—that is until the fire's discipline works out our carnality and we're walking in greatness. Then our characters are forged like tungsten steel in the image of Christ, and we're left unshakable, immovable, and always abounding in the work of God.

God setting our life on fire is pretty simple.

If God's gotta hang with us, then He wants us in holy shape. He wants our characters to reflect His. How many of you have that friend or family member who embarrasses you? What do you do with them—especially if they're family? You can't kill them. So, you start to shape them up. Sometimes it hurts their feelings; sometimes it hurts their flesh. For instance, if they're grossly overweight or addicted to heroin, it's going to be a climb aboard the pain train for them to become a free bird. Some of us try to help our friends and family from our own altruistic motives, but most of us do it simply because we wanna look cool and our chunky-butt sister, who checks for wedgies in the buffet line, is just an embarrassment. God is similar, except of course, He's minus the sinful reasons we do things. Check it out.

The Scripture talks about some Christians who He's not ashamed to call brothers. (See Hebrews 2:11.) Which presupposes that there are a bunch He has on His Facebook network's *limited profile* because they are bizarre. To cure us miscreants who humiliate Him, He must shape us up, and the element He uses change our ways is not earth, not wind, but fire.

How many folks do you know who, after some cataclysmic crap in their lives, became better people? What happened? The trial purged all the bollocks from their hearts and minds and in the BS's place, they gained a new perspective, a selfless spirit, a godly focus, which drastically altered the path of their lives.

Please note that it didn't happen when they were on top of the world. It didn't happen in a cool swimming pool, drinking a *mojito*, but shaking and baking in a 2400-degree kiln. I don't know about you, but I tend to forget God when I'm Von Trapping on a mountaintop, but have a tendency to remember Him while schlepping through Death Valley.

The bottom line is this: if we're God's kids, then He's going to spank our backsides to get us to produce what He likes, and as stated, He likes His Son and He wants to see *His* reflection in the mirror of our lives. Yep, God disciplines His children. Sure, He'll use the carrot; but He has no problem whatsoever using the stick.

Nowadays, a lot of parents don't discipline their little angels and consequently they morph into little Damiens. You've seen these undisciplined, demonic children, haven't you? The screaming little brats, cursing like Denis Leary would if he ran out of cigarettes, coffee, and just smacked his *cojones* with a hammer. Since we blew off disciplining our rug rats, we now have kids on leashes who look like sugared-up, rabid Rotties intent on breaking stuff. Yea, veritable feral youth who have to have new diseases invented to explain away their revolting behavior, which is a direct result of not having their butts lit up.

God's skooch is different with His spiritual kids than today's dilatory parental units. He will not have an undisciplined, freak kid like the above careening around the neighborhood causing chaos, making everything suck for everybody, all the while giving God a bad name. Oh, no. God will whup that kid's butt. He will allow life to squeeze that little one into righteousness.

You see, *Yahweh* has no prescription meds to feed His rogue children who have HADD—*Heavenly Attention Deficit Disorder.* No, He has a belt, He has a kiln, a fire to put us through to shape our spirit up and He is not afraid to baptize us in it. Matter of fact, He'll discipline some so thoroughly that one can come real close to passing out.

Check it out here:

My son, do not regard lightly the discipline of the Lord, nor faint when you are reproved by him; for those whom the Lord loves he disciplines, and he scourges every son who he receives.

It is for discipline that you endure; God deals with you as with sons; for what son is there whom his father does not discipline?

But if you are without discipline, of which all have become partakers, then you are illegitimate children and not sons.

Furthermore, we had earthly fathers to discipline us, and we respected them; shall we not much rather be subject to the Father of spirits, and live?

For they disciplined us for a short time as seemed best to them, but He disciplines us for our good, so that we may share His holiness.

All discipline for the moment seems not to be joyful, but sorrowful; yet to those who have been trained by it, afterwards it yields the peaceful fruit of righteousness. (Hebrews 12:5-11, NASB)

So, quickly, what does the writer say about discipline?

• "Don't regard discipline lightly." If you're getting your clock cleaned and God's addressing your character, then don't blow Him off; pay close attention, because, yes, things can get worse. Way worse.

• "Don't faint." Once again, here's a little ditty that you'll never hear on Christian TV or radio or in sappy Christian music ... namely, that God's discipline can be so intense that one can come close to fainting. Cowboy up, girlfriend. You're not going to die. Yet.

• "Discipline = Love." Postmodern autoerotic narcissists view right and wrong by pleasure and pain. If it's "right and good," it will give me pleasure and gumdrops. If it's "wrong and bad," it will cause me pain. Well, I hate to break it to you,

Perez Hilton, but God is holy, just, and good, and He'll enact painful discipline upon you to wake you the heck up—all because He loves you.

- "No discipline, no Heaven." The King James Version of this text says if you are undisciplined, then you're a bastard. That ain't nice, now is it? It might not be nice, but it is God. So … does your spiritual butt bear Heaven's stripes? If not, I hope you like hot cavernous environs, the eternal smell of sulfur, and are completely comfy with demonic spirits because that's where you're headed.

- "Subject yourself to the discipline" when it comes. When my mom and dad use to whip my backside for being Doug, I did everything I could to not be spanked. I ran, I cried, I promised, I swore. I did everything except subject myself to the reason, the lesson, behind the discipline. So, guess what? I got pummeled again and again for my lack of subjugation. You see, I wanted the pain to stop. I was not interested in subjecting myself to their rules or wisdom. My point? Learn the lesson rather than try to escape the pain. Trust me, the pain will subside when the lesson is learned. Or you can stubbornly plow on and see what happens. I'm betting you'll lose.

- "This is going to suck." Discipline (the fire) will not be joyful. You know why? Because all discipline sucks. Discipline is different from ice cream. The only way to milk joy out of this crap storm you're in is to look to the promises within the Scripture regarding what God will do for those who yield to life's flames and hang on to those promises like a tenacious little monkey. Don't let go.

- "You'll share His character." This is freaky. Via el fuego we become partakers of His holiness, His character, wisdom, person, and works. Unbelievable, eh? What's so unbelievable, you ask? It's mind-boggling, at least to me, that radically corrupt critters like us are actually allowed, in a limited sense, to share a thrice-holy God's nature and attributes, that's what. If that's not stunning to you then you have a low view of who

God is and a high view of who you are, which officially makes you a fool.

• "Fire equals fruit." Professional hunters in Africa and elsewhere will occasionally conduct controlled burns on the property they hunt. These purposeful flames produce the removal of thick underbrush, which makes the hunted animals difficult to see. It also produces fresh grass for the animals to feast upon. According to the above text, the discipline of God is a fruit-producer. Sometimes—a lot of times—the only way God can get "new grass" in our lives, both in quality and quantity, is to burn down to the ground that which currently exists. Here's where you've got to trust that when God takes something away, He always has something new, fresh, and amazing up His sleeve, even though in the moment you cannot see it or understand it.

King David, the warrior poet, Dove award winner, and giant slayer said that going through hell taught him to not go astray. (See Psalm 119:67; 71; 75.).

We can get cocky as Christians and think we can stray from God's prescribed path, play with sin, and still be a cool, yummy Christian. Davey said pain, affliction, and God taking him to the holy woodshed dissuaded him of that notion. Oh yes, it wasn't the sweet presence of precious Jesus, but affliction leveled by a holy God that shaped his butt up and caused him to sit up and pay attention to God's way versus his wants.

Matter of fact, David, man of perspective that he was, said that after several life/butt beatings it was actually good that he went through hell because it taught him things about God like no seminary could. (See Psalm 119:71.) David said that God showed His faithfulness to him, not just by giving him puppy dogs and candy canes, but also by afflicting him when he went loopy and thought he could get away with his adultery and murder.

So, why the hard times?

Why the difficulties?

Well, according to Hebrews, according Malachi, it's about our character, Stupid. And the sooner we embrace life's flames, the quicker we learn the lesson and get out of life's smelting pot.

At least for a little while.

Chapter Four

The Three Sources of "Hell"

From what I've deduced from the Scriptures, there are three major sources of hell for us generic sinners. They are: loud chicks on cell phones, the Department of Motor Vehicles, and broccoli. All right, maybe those aren't the top three sources of pain, but they're way up there. Nope, from the Scriptures the top three prongs from which personal pain proceeds are:

Us.

Satan.

God.

Identifying the source of the shizzle helps to field the funk causing us to overcome the junk (I'm about to start rappin' ...), once the source is determined and understood. Yep, if we can do the math regarding who is doing what to us, then we can react appropriately and mitigate the hell. We can even grow through the pain and, believe it or not, nancy boys, actually overcome the fiery trial when it hits our lives. Imagine that: Christians actually winning in life.

Does that sound tasty?

It does to me.

Let me explain the *tres amigos* of pain.

Us

And Nathan said to David, "Thou art the man" … And David said unto Nathan, "I have sinned against the LORD." (2 Samuel 12:7;13, KJV)

My default fault page for the horse hockey in my life is *moi.* Yep, I blame me.

Not others.

Not the Devil.

Not God.

Not the liberals.

Not the oppressive "man" or "the machine."

Not my inner child.

Not a devil woman.

Not the siren song of filthy lucre.

Not the vexing power of a sinful city.

Not *Playboy.*

Not *Fortune Magazine.*

Not *Guns & Ammo.*

Not billboards with sexy girls pictured.

Not Corona.

Not Johnny Walker Blue, Black, or Red Label.

Not the amazing bullcrap a slick politician can spin.

And not the bad drivers down here in south Florida. (Y'know who I'm talking about, don't you? The hideous drivers who make me go absolutely insane with their unbelievable horrible vehicular practices, antics, and violations. Curse you bad drivers, curse you!)

Oops.

Sorry about that.

I kinda lost it there.

Whew.

I got in the flesh.

I've gotta calm down.

Serenity now.

I've gotta breathe.

Inhale. Exhale. Inhale. Exhale. In through the nose. Out through the mouth.

Okay.

Serenity now.

I'm back.

Yes, I blame me for the problems in my life. It is me—goofy, sin bent, God retardant, selfish, and self deceived dorkus maximus, little old me who has courted disaster and invited demons to my castle.

If the truth can still be told, I, Doug Giles, Dumb Ass Emeritus—and I use the word "ass" in the biblical sense (see Job 11:12, KJV)—created most of the pain in my life that I have had to plow through. I should say all of the pain, but I still have some reservoirs of self-love within my soul. Help me, Sam Vaknin!

Now don't get me wrong all you dysfunctional blame shifters, I'd love to fault others for the pain in my life. I'd love to blame Lucifer, or my parents who didn't cater to my dream of being the center of the universe, or my low blood sugar which caused me to rob several convenience stores, or heck … I wouldn't even mind faulting God for the painful parts of my *mi vida*. However, if I must be honest, which, since I'm a Christian, I guess I have to be, I must come clean and admit that I spawned most of the monsters that I have had to deal with. I'd love to join the pusillanimous, responsibility-dodging pack, but it just sounds so pathetically dishonest and oh, so lame, when a whiner plays the card of blame.

Check it out.

When I've stumbled into iniquity (read "jumped"), it was because I blew off about fifty different checks and balances from God, His Word, common sense, and true friends. It wasn't "the Devil who made me do it;" it was Doug, Dumb Ass Emeritus, who both inspired the sin and then sowed the dirty deed and is thus *responsible* for the harvest from hell.

FYI—the word *responsible* is an antiquated attitude and action that was once commonplace in a prosperous and righteous American milieu. For those who have never heard of the term/concept here is Dictionary.com's definition of this now foreign notion:

Re-spon-si-ble [ri-**spon**-*suh-buh*l]—*adjective* 1. answerable or accountable, as for something within one's power, control, or management (often fol. by *to* or *for*). 2. involving accountability or responsibility: a responsible position. 3. chargeable with being the author, cause, or occasion of something (usually fol. by for): termites were responsible for the damage. 4. having a capacity for moral decisions and therefore accountable; capable of rational thought or action.

Harvard sociologist professor Dr. Full O'Krappe states that since the advent of Sigmund Freud, Jerry Springer, Rikki Lake, and metrosexuality, responsibility has been seen and heard less and less in our families, churches, and within our government. Tragically, responsibility is now on our culture's endangered virtue list.

Is there anyone else out there who's absolutely, radically, and fundamentally pig sick of hearing preening preachers, carpy Christians, Hollywood tarts, and greasy, sinister, can't-scrape-'em-off-your-shoes politicians pass the blame to other people, places, and things that should land squarely on their own shoulders?

Huh?

No doubt, some of you are thinking, "But doesn't Satan tempt us to sin and doesn't he bring demonic disaster, pressure, and persecution to Christians?" Yes, honey, he does. And I'll talk about that in detail in *uno momento*. But you know what? *El Diablo* gets blamed for a ton of smack that is our own wicked heart's fault and not his. We've been doing that blame game ever since Adam and Eve blew God off in the garden when Eve blamed the serpent and Adam blamed Eve *and* God! (See Genesis 3.) And the wheels of the bus go 'round and 'round, 'round and 'round ...

The more things change, the more they stay the same, eh?

Look, Homeslice, if Satan, *Penthouse*, Glenlivet, money, and Miami did not exist, our wicked hearts would find plenty of goo to get into all by their little lonesomes. God could chain Satan up like a dog, and without his diabolical influence upon thy soul you and I would still act ... like a dog. The reason? Well, we're human, and being human we have this little thing called a corrupt, constituent nature that does not need a seminar on how to sin or an unclean spirit to entice us, for that nature is, according to Christ, a source and a supply of sin and disaster in and of itself.

> *For out of the heart proceed evil thoughts, murders, adulteries, fornications, thefts, false witness, blasphemies.* (Matthew 15:19, KJV)

The seventeenth century Puritan Thomas Brooks put it this way:

> Satan hath a persuading sleight, not an enforcing might. He may tempt us, but without ourselves he cannot conquer us; he may entice us, but without

ourselves he cannot hurt us. Our hearts carry the greatest stroke in every sin. Satan can never undo a man without himself; but a man may easily undo himself without Satan ... therefore do the Devil so much right, as not as to excuse yourselves, by your accusing him, and laying the load upon him, that you should lay upon your hearts.

The key to getting out of the self-inflicted, hellish nightmare we are embroiled in is to first and foremost take responsibility for our own ridiculousness. If we broke the commandments of God, if we blew off common sense, if we took out a mortgage we couldn't afford, or married a person we never should have, or didn't raise our kids with TLC, don't you think we sound and look a little loopy when we point the finger at others, be they material or immaterial beings? We were the ones who did the dirty deed. What in heck did we think was going to happen? Did we imagine that somehow, magically, God would morph our horrendously selfish and bad decisions into a box of Lucky Charms with yellow moons and green clovers? The Scriptures are clear that we will reap what we sow. If we sow stupidity, we'll reap stupid.

> *Do not be deceived, God is not mocked; for whatever a man sows, this he shall also reap. For the one who sows to his own flesh shall from the flesh reap corruption, but the one who sows to the Spirit will from the Spirit reap eternal life.* (Galatians 6:7-8, NASB)

The great men and women of the Bible, when busted by the trials in life that they spawned, didn't fault bad leaders, naughty friends, Paris Hilton, Lucifer, or Yahweh, but instead said something like this, "I have sinned and done what is evil in Thy sight (Psalm 51) and I completely understand why I'm having my clock cleaned right now. Please forgive me and have mercy on my mucked up life" or something to that effect.

I suggest we do the same …

Satan

There are two equal and opposite errors into which we can fall about the devils. One is to disbelieve in their existence. The other is to believe, and to feel an excessive and unhealthy interest in them. —C.S. Lewis

Man, am I about to sound like a non-evolved, Pentecostal, snake-handling throwback to the Salem witch-burning days, because I believe, God forgive me, that there is a literal Devil and literal demons that us mortals, in particularly Christians, have to contend with.

Call me medieval. I'm cool with that.

To be clear, I don't believe Lucifer is a pitchfork-sporting, cloven-hoofed, little dude in a red-hooded unitard, with two modest horns on top of his goatee-bearded head who runs around poking people in the butt with his trident. I believe he's more stealthy than that. I also believe he looks more like Nancy Pelosi than he does Sully Erna, but that's just me.

Simply put, if you truly believe the Bible, then no matter how uncool and kooky it sounds in this oh, so sassy secularized day, you must believe that there is a hell, a Devil, and that there are demons and they will be around running the DNC 'til the end of time. Sorry, I mean, they will try to derail the purpose of God until the end of time. You would have to edit the Scripture to believe otherwise.

FYI—This book is not an apologetic for the existence of *el Diablo*. If you don't believe in his existence then there's nothing I can do to convince you. Life will have to teach you. I like life to tutor people. I'm a nice guy and I hate shoving biblical truths down people's throats. I'd rather let them have their smarmy, atheistic beliefs that they learned at the feet of their clove-smoking, long-toothed, atheistic, lesbian philosophy professor at some junior college.

Yep, I'd rather have them embrace anti-God rhetoric for a couple of decades and see how that works out for them. Y'know, give the whole "God is a lie" a good test run. C'mon atheists, go for it. Matter of fact, if I were you I would do the exact opposite of what the Bible says. If there is no God and the Bible is a bunch of crap, then if I were an atheist I would do the reverse of what it purports, and borrow zero capital from its supposed inspired pages. Go ahead, give it a whirl and get back to me regarding how you're doing via an email at mail@ You'reDepressedAndHopelessAren'tYou.com

Anyway, with some know-it-alls, the only thing that will bring them around to believe in God and the Scripture is when they take the big dirt nap and, low and behold, they find out that they were dead wrong about the whole God thing. And now the God they disbelieved in has sent them to the hell that they knew didn't exist and has put them right beside the Devil who they thought was a figment of foolish Christians' imaginations. Oops.

Now, back to my point about Satan being a purveyor of pain to the Christian.

According to the Bible, saints can experience hell on Earth from Old Slew-foot because they're kicking butt and taking names for God. A righteous life does not exclude a believer from the blunt end of hell's pool cue. Matter of fact, it guarantees it. Hello.

Question: What happened to Jesus right after He was baptized and He and His parents went to eat the Falafel Fun Lunch Special at that Denny's overlooking the Jordan River?

Did the heavens part again and candy canes cascade down upon Him from the Father of Lights? No.

Did Oprah ask Him on her show to talk about what it feels like to be the product of a hypostatic union?

No.

Did the FOX execs, because of the obvious celestial favor and JC's national popularity, invite Him to do a weekly family-friendly reality show with good moral values called *Jamming with Jesus*? Wrong again, Monkey Man.

What happened was, and I hate to bring the Bible into this, but according to Luke 4:1-13, Jesus spent the next forty days and forty nights having Satan work Him over like a peckish dog gnaws a bone, that's what.

Oh, and by the way. When Jesus went toe-to-toe with Satan, believe it or not, He didn't cave in because things were "so hard." In addition, Jesus did not renounce God and become a Buddhist, sleep with two candy girls, or give in and smoke a big hookah stuffed full of blond Lebanese hash because of the overwhelming demonic attacks. No, on the contrary, He beat Lucifer at his own game and He did it on a very, very, very empty stomach. Hoorah.

Gentle Jesus, meek and mild?

I don't think so.

Now, if you listen to the schlock on Christian television you'd get the idea that saints don't suffer at the hand of the Devil—but the Bible says they do.

> *Be sober, be vigilant; because your adversary the devil, as a roaring lion, walketh about, seeking whom he may devour: Whom resist stedfast in the faith, knowing that the same afflictions are accomplished in your brethren that are in the world. But the God of all grace, who hath called us unto his eternal glory by Christ Jesus, after that ye have suffered a while, make you perfect, stablish, strengthen, settle you.* (1 Peter 5:8-10, KJV)

Given the fact that believers will be attacked, they can do one of two things: one, they can fall on the floor, roll up in the fetal position, suck their thumbs, and wet their big Christian diapers; or two, they can put on the full armor of God (see Ephesians 6:10-18) and go to war against the works of darkness. I recommend war, ladies.

> *Finally, be strong in the Lord and in the strength of His might. Put on the full armor of God, that you may be able to stand firm against the schemes of the devil. For our struggle is not against flesh and blood, but against the rulers, against the powers, against the world forces of this darkness, against the spiritual forces of wickedness in the heavenly places. Therefore, take up the full armor of God, that you may be able to resist in the evil day, and having done everything, to stand firm.* (Ephesians 6:10-13, NASB)

The biblical answer to any and all demonic attacks is … attack back! Matter of fact, get on the offense in this holy war. Don't wait for the demonic hosts to throttle you. You—hello!—garrote them. Throw the first punch. Solicit their wrath versus waiting for it. Use the spiritual weapons God has equipped you with and fish slap the sons of monkeys first thing in the morning. Can you dig it?

If a person has a hunger and thirst for God, you can bet your backside that the powers of darkness are going to harass that cat more than Rosie would abuse her PA who is thirty minutes late with a case of Twinkies for her afternoon snack.

The operative word/phrase above that draws the Devil's arrows is "hunger and thirst for God." Which translates: you are following God and loving His Word and ways as much as a dorky sinner can. In other words, you're not a casual Christian, one of those non-zealous religious slugs who moves like a manatee high on North Slope devil crotch skunk weed, swimming in heavy tractor oil in the intensified gravitational pull of planet Pluto. (Is Pluto still a planet?)

Anyway, you're not a dull Christian who the pastor has to put a strobe light next to during church to make you stay awake and look alive for the Sunday service. No, the one who solicits Satan and his ilk's ill will is the Scotty-on-fire friend of God who is on top of the things of Christ like stink on a monkey.

Reality: If you're an earnest believer then you will draw hellfire as Jesus did. (See below.)

> *And the dragon stood before the woman who was about to give birth, so that when she gave birth he might devour her child. And she gave birth to a son, a male child, who is to rule all the nations with a rod of iron; and her child was caught up to God and to His throne.* (Revelation 12:4-5, NASB)

Why did Jesus attract hell's fury? He was a threat, and since you are a threat to the powers of darkness, their goal is to forever make your life suck until you blow off the pursuit of God and just simply become a tame and tepid Christmas and Easter Christian, the kind that cannot pray the fuzz off a peach.

I, on the other hand, would rather be run over by a Mac truck than live a carefree, "nice" life, being ignored by the forces of hell. Drawing fire into one's existence from *el Diablo* is quite the honor. It means you're on hell's radar. You are over the target. You are a liability. They want to hinder you because when you're awake, praying, and obeying, you are a big pain in their devil butt and what solid saint would not want to be that? Think of the people in the Scriptures that Satan jacked with. It wasn't the non-threatening, spiritual Chihuahuas, the Dudley Paunch Guts of Christendom, who didn't give a flip about God and man, but rather the soul savers, nation changers, and dragon slayers who were the ones who courted the dragon's wrath.

As far as God is concerned, it is an honor to be badgered by the horned one.

So, what kind of attacks can the believer expect from our enemy?

What kind of hell will hell put us through?

Here's a short list.

• Expect weird, demonic attraction to sin. Not a normal magnetism for sin, but the abnormal, "this has got to be Satan inspired" sort of aberrant tugs toward evil. (See Acts 5:3.)

• Expect all kinds of hellish hassles trying to keep you from doing what is right. When you were an unmotivated dork, you had no problems. Once you became an awakened saint who wants nothing more than to follow God with all your heart, soul, mind, and strength, everything is frickin' hard. (See 1 Corinthians 16:9.)

• Expect the powers of darkness to keep bringing up past failures and present weaknesses and keep you in a condemned, guilt-ridden state of mind. Guilt and condemnation is the soup de jour hell's kitchen serves on a millennial basis because it is so effective in sidelining Christians from pursuing the purposes of God in life because of feelings of unworthiness. (See Revelation 12:10.) That's one thing Satan is right on with; we're not worthy. True dat! We will never be worthy. It's called grace, folks. Realize it. Live it. Love it.

• Expect him to throw all kinds of doubts and fears in the zealous one's life and hamstring that one with unbelief. It's faith that moves mountains. Therefore, you can bet your backside that the powers of darkness are going to slap the godly with more doubts than Christopher Hitchens has watching a TBN Praise-a-Thon. (See 1 Chronicles 21:1.)

• Expect to be ridiculed for your faith, not be invited to parties, lose your friends, your slutty girlfriend (or boyfriend!) doesn't like you anymore, you might be fired from your job, and there is always the possibility of physical beatings, prison, and even death. (See Acts 7:55-59.)

And that's just a smidgen of the smack you and I can anticipate from hell's CEO and his corporate clowns. But it ain't no big thang. The worst they can do to you is kill you. And if they kill you, they just send you to Heaven sooner—to the place where you get many distinct celestial pleasures. One of them being that you never, ever have to see or hear the chicks on *The View* again! Never.

Just like self-inflicted pain can cease when we stop beating ourselves up, demonic attacks can be curtailed as well. So if you find yourself being hammered by the enemy, what do you do? I used to go to a crazy charismatic church that did elaborate things to ward off demonic attacks. I know I'm not proud of it. They would do stuff like screaming in tongues, yelling at the Devil, singing, dancing, exorcisms—it was a freak fest. One thing that I noticed was that most of the people stayed demonized. Yeah, it didn't seem to work. Why didn't it work for them when those various things have worked, and will work, for others? I deduced why it did not work for them down to the conviction that they were disobedient, and when you're disobedient God doesn't fight your battles. I knew most of these goofballs and they did everything right except live an upright life. Hey, dimwit Christian, you can bind the Devil all day long but if you embrace the lust of the flesh, the lust of the eyes, and the boastful pride of life, don't expect the Jesus who rejected all that crap to prop your haggard butt up just because you're singing a Michael W. Smith song and are dancing in place.

Spiritual warfare ain't complicated, ladies and gents. Obey God and when Satan hits you, God will rise to defend you and, last time I checked, He's purty darn good at opening up a big can of whoop-ass.

I know this doesn't sound sexy for charismatic/Pentecostal Christians who love to scream, sing and shout at demons, and do "spiritual warfare," but if one is simply obedient to the commandments of God, then God fights your battles. If you're not going to obey His Word then I hope you like toast, because that's what you're about to become—toast!

The Scripture is full of examples of God's disobedient people who sang, shouted, and got all lathered up and confident that they're were going to kick some enemy butt only to get their backside beaten by the enemy (Exhibit A: 1 Samuel 4:1-22). Why? Well, it was because they were disobedient darlings who imagined they could blow God off in life and that He would back them when they needed Him. How quaint. Ain't gonna happen, Cha Cha.

Sorry, but God isn't a faucet you can turn on and off. God didn't back His people when they were contumacious. When the enemy came against them, they got hassled like Don Wildmon would at a Lil Wayne concert. God's message to them in their demon thrashing: If you want My protection and deliverance, you've got to jump through My hoops. You've got to trust and obey or you'll rust and decay.

It goes something like this . . .

Simpletons! How long will you wallow in ignorance? Cynics! How long will you feed your cynicism? Idiots! How long will you refuse to learn? About face! I can revise your life. Look, I'm ready to pour out my spirit on you; I'm ready to tell you all I know. As it is, I've called, but you've turned a deaf ear; I've reached out to you, but you've ignored me. Since you laugh at my counsel and make a joke of my advice, how can I take you seriously? I'll turn the tables and joke about your troubles! What if the roof falls in, and your whole life goes to pieces? What if catastrophe strikes and there's nothing to show for your life but rubble and ashes? You'll need me then. You'll call for me, but don't expect an answer. No matter how hard you look, you won't find me. Because you hated Knowledge and had nothing to do with the Fear-of-God, because you wouldn't take my advice and brushed aside all my offers to train you, well, you've made your bed—now lie in it; you wanted your own way—now, how do you like it? Don't you see what happens, you simpletons, you idiots? Carelessness kills; complacency is murder. First pay attention to me, and then relax. Now you can take it easy—you're in good hands. (Proverbs 1:22-33, MSG)

By the way, I didn't write that. Solomon did via inspiration of the Holy Spirit. I'll bet you 10.3 trillion dollars that you have never heard that chunk of Scripture preached in your church. Any takers?

In contrast with God not defending His rebel kids in battle, He also promises insane protection for His obedient people no matter what comes against them to destroy them. For instance ...

If ye walk in my statutes, and keep my commandments, and do them; I will give peace in the land, and ye shall lie down, and none shall make you afraid: and I will rid evil beasts out of the land, neither shall the sword go through your land. And five of you shall chase an hundred, and an hundred of you shall put ten thousand to flight: and your enemies shall fall before you by the sword. And ye shall chase your enemies, and they shall fall before you by the sword. (Leviticus 26:3; 6-8, KJV)

In the Old Testament God took great pleasure in letting His people become ridiculously outnumbered and outgunned by the enemy, and then utterly whip those adversaries with ridiculous methods and means. Their victory was based not in His tribe's physical might and power, but rather in their obedience to and faith in Him. Do you need an example? Here is one among many. Check this stuff out.

Exodus 14: The children of Israel, who had no Uzis, no stealth fighters, no Bradley tanks, who did not know Jiu Jitsu, or how to toss Chinese throwing stars, or use nunchucks, who were tired, overworked slaves and had only their two bare feet for transport, got chased by Pharaoh and his estimated 1.5-5.5 million man army. They were pursued to a beach and jammed up against a coastline and were told to do two things by Moses if they wanted to defeat Pharaoh. Namely—stand and shut up. That's it. Stand. And shut up. Nothing fancy. Just stand and shut up. As they stood and zipped it, God parted the sea and they ran through on dry land. What happened to Pharaoh and his funky bunch, well, it didn't go that well for them. God drowned them all in the Red Sea. Dee-licious. Behold, the weird things God does to our enemies when we simply obey.

Obedience is the highest form of spiritual warfare....

God

God has not been trying an experiment on my faith or love in order to find out their quality. He knew it already. It was I who didn't. In this trial He makes us occupy the dock, the witness box, and the bench all at once. He always knew my temple was a house of cards. His only way of making me realize the fact was to knock it down. —C.S. Lewis

Lastly, I guarantee you haven't heard this ditty much in our dilatory churches: God will, for His good purpose, toss His kids into divine darkness and inexplicable trials simply to stretch them for His own purposes.

This can be "hellish" as well to our *carne*.

This God-sent, purpose-driven storm is for the purpose-driven life. In this tempest you can pray, repent, bind the Devil, and go to church thirty times a week, and yet it won't go away. This "hell" is brutal in that it is not because of sin, but because of an intended use He has in mind for the benefit of not only you, but also for others in the future. Moses, David, Joseph, Job, and a host of others know what I'm talking about. The key to this tsunami is to lay low, get content with His weird dealings, and just worship Him.

So, how do you know if it is God who is stretching you like a rappelling rope with Larry the Cable Guy on the end of it? Well, if you repent and take responsibility, if you obey and resist the Devil to the best of your fallen ability, and the trial doesn't come to an end, then it is probably God putting you through a weird experiment to test your calling, conviction, and commitment to Him and His purpose. Yeah, maybe He thinks you're a fair weather Christian. One thing is for certain. He'll road test you before He puts you out on the street.

> *Bless our God, O peoples! Give him a thunderous welcome! Didn't he set us on the road to life? Didn't he keep us out of the ditch? He trained us first, passed us like silver through refining fires, brought us into hardscrabble country, pushed us to our very limit, **road-tested us inside and out, took us to hell and back; finally he brought us to this well-watered place.*** (Psalm 66:8-12, MSG, emphasis mine)

Chapter Five

Solomon Says, "Relax"

EVERYONE FEELS BENEVOLENT IF NOTHING HAPPENS TO
BE ANNOYING HIM AT THE MOMENT. —C.S. LEWIS

Solomon states in the book of Ecclesiastes that one of the keys to surviving the brutalities of life is to relax ... chill ... drink some wine ... recreate ... and have a good laugh. And according to some scholars, Solomon didn't say that at the beginning of his prodigal period when he went off the rails on a crazy train with the idols and the concubines and stuff. No, this advice was at the end of his life when he had already experienced massive highs and debasing lows. It was after he had penned the Proverbs, written the Song of Songs, departed from God, and had come back to reality. Then he summed up life as vanity in which one would do well to ... first, fear the Lord (see Ecclesiastes 12:13); second, enjoy the ride; and third, drink some wine. In other words, keep it simple, Stupid. Eugene Petersen put it this way:

> *Seize life! Eat bread with gusto,*
> *Drink wine with a robust heart.*

Oh yes—God takes pleasure in your pleasure!
Dress festively every morning.
Don't skimp on colors and scarves.
Relish life with the spouse you love each and every day of your precarious life.
Each day is God's gift. It's all you get in exchange for the hard work of staying alive.
Make the most of each one!
Whatever turns up, grab it and do it. And heartily!
This is your last and only chance at it, for there's neither work to do nor thoughts to think in the company of the dead, where you're most certainly headed.
(Ecclesiastes 9:7-10, MSG)

I'm sure most Christians get the "everything is vanity" stuff from Sol's pen. I'm certain most of the faithful get the "life is hard work, a sweat of the brow," subsistence advice. (Except, of course, the metrosexual, thirty-year-old, evangelical males who live with mommy and won't get a job.) I am also equally positive that most sincere Christians understand the crucial requirement of the fear of God for worship and wellbeing.

But relaxing?

Enjoying the ride?

Seizing life?

And wine?

Drinking wine?

Giles, have you gone nuts? Yes, I have and I'm loving every minute of it. Christians aren't supposed to drink alcohol, Christians aren't supposed to laugh their butts off, Christians aren't supposed to lighten up, dial down, and smell the roses. We're 'sposed to be a high strung, nerve grating, everything is a five alarm fire bunch of people loaded down with stress and anxiety "for the Lord," right? Wrong, Dinky. Dead wrong. And here's a little ditty: if you don't chill and chill soon, you will soon be … dead.

When one begins to go through the meat grinder of life, the first thing to vanish like a pack of Camels at a crack house is … joy. Joy is serious business because, according to God, without it you're oh, so lame. You and I won't be able to stand against the forces of hell, our rotten desires, or endure God's discipline without getting happy in the Lord.

Yep, without the gravity-defying virtue of joy cranking through our spirits we won't be able to pray through a wet paper sack. Fickle and vapid Christians disobey the command to rejoice in all things—and God means *all* things—and this includes all non-yippee stuff. Consequently, such sad saints don't transcend their transient trials, and God has no other recourse but to send them around the mountain again until they learn the power of laughing their butts off in the face of adversity.

> *This day is holy to God. Don't feel bad. The joy of God is your strength!" The Levites calmed the people, "Quiet now. This is a holy day. Don't be upset." So the people went off to feast, eating and drinking and including the poor in a great celebration. Now they got it; they understood the reading that had been given to them.* (Nehemiah 8:10b-12, MSG)

So what do I suggest one does when wrapped around the axle of life and about to stroke out? I suggest what I do; namely, I start hunting joy. As stated above, the joy of the Lord is our strength. Without it we're doomed to fail. And not only without it are we destined to eat dirt, but we're also a pain in the butt to all who know us because we're sad, mean, and ugly little monkeys to everyone on our way down.

Doesn't that sound great?

Sad, mean, and ugly little monkeys for Jesus.

Yes, when I have been saddled with smack and I'm becoming a depressed little pitiful waa-waa wonk who is getting moody "working, fighting, and living for God" … I quickly get off my couch and haul my skinny butt down to Blockbuster and get a Ben Stiller movie to shake the depressed fog off my backside before I start going Kurt Cobain.

Life is intense, folks, and no one can live at high RPM's, 24/7/365 without a spring blowin' out of the side of their noggin. Even church stuff can make you go insane. I'm probably going to sound like a heretic but some of you guys have got to get off the religious merry-go-round and lighten the heck up. If you're in a "bad place," then more than likely it is going to take awhile to get out of the hell that you're in. If you didn't get into it overnight, then more than likely you're not going to get out of it overnight. Therefore, in the meantime, in between time, you have to relax.

I find it really interesting that Jesus safeguarded His soul by going to the mountains, boating, fishing, get around people in the market place, chillin' with His boys, hanging at parties, and eating and drinking with the best of them. He ate and drank so much He was beginning to get a rep that He was a glutton and a lush. (See Matthew 11:19, MSG.) Yes, Virginia, Jesus was anything but a weepy, ascetic, moody, and pouty lone wolf, vapid monk.

What follows is what I do to get the Churchillian "black dog" from nippin' at my backside. This is my trip. My salvo. These are my vents and liberties. To each his own. What you do to blow off steam is between you and Hey-Soos. Since I am writing this book and you're not, I'm going to tell you what I do and why I do it without telling you to do the same.

Hunting

We need to conserve that bitter impulse that we have inherited from primitive man. It alone permits us the greatest luxury of all, the ability to enjoy a vacation from the human condition through an authentic, "immersion in Nature" … and this, in turn, can be achieved only by placing himself in relation to another animal. But there is no animal, pure animal, other than a wild one, and the relationship with him is the hunt. –Jose Ortega y Gasset

As a columnist, minister, and talk-show host, my job entails (and I love it) ticking off as many vapid, anti-American, and anti-traditional values blowhards as I can. It is one of the chief joys of my life. However, sometimes I need a reprieve from the rancor and the hell-*razing*.

Aside from needing a break from the bellicosity that is my life, I need a break from the place where I live, i.e., Miami. This place is more plastic than Joan River's face, bosom, ear lobes, tummy, or … yack! I'm sorry. I just made myself gag.

Excuse me for a sec …

Okay, I'm back.

In addition to the synthetic scene in South Florida, the metrosexual madness down here is so sassy and solid it leaves a redneck refugee like me shaking like a junkie for a testosterone reality fix away from the weapons-grade foolishness that unfortunately inundates one of the most beautiful spots on the planet.

Also, I get ill thinking about having to go to the mall, again, and having to ford through all the mall rats, with their fake (or real, I don't care) Louis Vuitton purses, Gucci shades, and their angst over, "whether they should get A/X's skinny jeans or Abercrombie's new ones." Yeah, having to share air with these helix-missing morons and being forced to overhear how their lives reek as they scream on their cell phones, leaves me with an intense desire to get the heck outta Dodge. Y'know what I'm sayin'?

Furthermore (and I know I'm not supposed to say this), I get weary at times of radio and TV talk shows, which are my life. Doesn't it get old, occasionally, hearing the left and right go at each other night after night after night after night? Call me a wussy, but since I don't drop acid or smoke ganja any more I need to escape.

A cruise is out of the question for me. Being on a disease-laden, slow-moving, Montezuma's revenge ship, filled with stretch-pants-wearing, buffet-loving, overweight, pink-skinned drunks that are paraded like lemmings from one overpriced port to the next is not my idea of recreating.

Nothing, as far as I'm concerned, does more for me than getting away and going hunting with my family and friends. Putting massive distance between me and the mall, my cell phone and email, and going beyond the pavement in pursuit of the planet's magnificent game animals or birds is b-e-a-u-tiful to me.

What do I like about it?

• My cell phone usually doesn't work.

• Just getting out in the wild connects me back to my primal spiritual and physical roots. God didn't create Adam to live in a condo. He made a feral crib for His first man to live and whup it up in with Eve. There is something that the undomesticated does to me that no Lysol disinfected, five star hotel or "amusement park" can provide.

Everybody say, Hotel! Motel! Holiday Inn!

Uh, not me.

Nope, I'm going hunting. You can go to Disneyland. I will go to Africa. I'm cool with that.

• Everything slows down. I'm forced to chill out. I'm not going mach 2 with my hair on fire. I'm forced to shut up and quit screaming. I'm forced to breathe, and the air I inhale in the woods is clean and not some germ-infested, stale, fart-loaded, re-circulated office oxygen. (I office out of my home.)

• My senses come alive and are taken to a higher level by pursuing my prey. My eyes, ears, nose, feet, and hands kick into gear like they don't when I'm sitting like a drooling, giggling, Corona-drinking zombie watching *Seinfeld* on my couch.

• Hunting makes me get disciplined. To be a successful hunter requires strictness. To shoot a rifle, shotgun, pistol, or bow accurately takes commitment. To successfully stalk a big game animal and make a clean and lethal shot takes additional dedication. To hunt dangerous game animals requires that I be a seriously focused little monkey. To sit quietly for hours takes Tibetan monk-like tenacity. To chase wild boar through a swamp, cougars over miles of desert mountains, and elk where the air is thinner than the plot line of *American Pie* means I've gotta work out during the week, or I'm going to be more lost than Kevin Federline reading Charles Krauthammer. The above *de rigueur* explains why I don't see too many crackheads on the hunting fields. My sport demands you have your act together.

• Hunting changes lives. I've seen it several times. I have seen bored adults and kids come alive when the hunt commences. I've watched idiots on drugs lay them down for good because they got a greater buzz hunting with good people than they did snorting crank with their butt-munch friends in Hialeah. BTW, for the too-cool teen or twenty-something who might not think hunting can be as thrilling as drugs, come with me and confront a three hundred and fifty pound, PO'ed wild boar, or come to the 'glades and hunt gators out of an air boat, or take a shot at a grizzly with a bow, or face up to a hippo out of the water with a double rifle. I guarantee that ecstasy, 'shrooms, and a crystal has never, can never, and will never give you the buzz that these situations will. You'll mess your pants. Give it a try, girlfriend. You'll be sweating like Ahmadinejad in church.

• Hunting causes me to connect with friends and family on a deeper level. Life's busy in the city. Sometimes, even the "good" relationships we have with friends and family are about as shallow as a creek during a Death Valley drought. The campfire allows for communication that you do not get when the idiot box is on and everyone is running in fifty different directions. If it weren't for my dad taking me hunting every year when I was a kid, I probably wouldn't really even know him (which might be a plus for him, but would be a huge minus for me). In addition, via hunting I feed hundreds of poor people with high protein, low fat, yummy flesh that comes from my fresh kills. I guarantee that me and just three of my hunting compadres feed way more hungry people through hunting than your typical group of a thousand bleeding heart, yarbling, anti-hunters ever have or will.

• Another perk to the hunting reprieve is there are very few loony liberals. Yes, an additional great blessing regarding hunting is that I seldom, if ever, run into secular, "progressive," pluralistic, relativistic, big-government-loving, anti-military, God and country hating leftists.

Yes, when I'm looking for a break I bound into the swamp, brush, or woods with gun or bow in hand in pursuit of one of our planet's amazing game animals. Nothing, absolutely nothing, restores my soul like everything that surrounds the sport of hunting with friends and family.

[Author's note: Ditto with regard to sport fishing. Nothing like an escape from the rancor by having my forearms lit up by a monster shark, sailfish, tarpon, amberjack, jack cravelle, snook, permit, bonefish, dolphin, or swordfish. Ah … fishing. One of the main perks of living in Miami: a glut of big game fish is a quarter of a mile from my back door. If you want to fish South Florida you must use my stellar Captain, Gavet Tutle at www.backformore.com. Tell him I sent you.]

My Name Is Doug and I Like Drawing

One of the things that I like about what I do to stymie my insanity (in order to be fully enjoyed) is that it demands a massive change from the grind that produces my stress. Especially my top two exorcists—hunting and painting. They require a set of skills and a way of thinking that is different from my madness of ministry, being an author, and a professional smart mouth. Hunting and painting to me aren't amusements; they are occupying passions that bring me deep satisfaction and relief from the other things that I equally dig, but get weary of obsessing about.

And that's the key to my decompression: diving into that which is different.

Yep, when I get into the hunting or painting groove, the part of my mind and soul that is about to tap out because of stress gets a reprieve by not engaging it in the way it is used for my main calling(s). You can wear out your brain by overuse, just like a body part or a pair of underwear. As a minister, I get burned out trying to save dunderheads from destroying their lives (case in point: I just called precious souls "dunderheads"!) and I get tired of reading old books about God, man, and Satan. I get drained fighting for, in my little way via my show and weekly column, the soul of our nation. All work and no play make Doug a dull and dangerous boy. I figured out about ten years ago that I ain't Jesus, and if I don't go out into the woods, or get on the water, or get behind a canvas on a regular basis and start splattering paint, then somebody is going to get hurt because I get weird.

When it comes to painting here's what I do to get into that happy place where I start seeing puppy dogs and candy canes instead of the red spots of "I'm freaking out here" rage or the black dog of depression:

• First and foremost, the home phone and the cell phone go off the hook. Period. Isn't it weird that when you get down to relaxing all of a sudden the phone rings? Screw phones. Phones are from hell. I don't want to talk to anyone about anything when I get into the painting groove. My wifey and *mi ninas* are put on full Doug protect mode: no calls, 'til daddy emerges from his studio lair bespeckled with Winsor & Newton oils, singing, and laughing. Having the phone off is a divergence from my daily grind. And God said, "This is good."

• Music: I've got to have music blaring while I'm slinging paint. And I hate to offend my Christian brethren, but while painting I don't listen to Michael W. Smith, but to 70s and 80s classic rock (the songs of my youth), some Buble, a little Simply Red, a splash of Robert Plant, and, of course, Godsmack. Yes, when I paint, I sing. Like at the top of my lungs. Like a happy Jack Sparrow cranked up on two bottles of pirate's rum, I croon. It's quite the sight. Imagine me with my crappy voice, painting an African lion, making up the lyrics to Maneater while out of my skull on oil paints and turpentine fumes. Here's what I have found: singing your butt off, even if you suck as a singer, is a major element of change that brings relief from stress. Except, of course, to your neighbors who have to listen to your singing, which may sound like the screeching of mating cats.

• Messy clothes: My painting attire consists of old A&F cargo military pants that are covered from the waist down with multi-colored paint smears that have been collecting for many years. I can't remember the last time I washed those pants. I think it was in 2005. These trousers might as well be a Spiderman costume because when I don those babies I experience a metamorphosis. As Frank Costanza said, I become a "Phoenix rising from Arizona." I morph. I turn into Nicolai Fechin, baby. I'm Picasso. I'm Ilya Repin. I'm Mickey Angelo. As far as a shirt goes, I don't wear one. No shirt. No shoes. No problem. By the end of the painting experience, I am a paint smeared African warrior on the plains of the Serengeti working on an elaborate cave drawing. Funkalicious. Let's get weird. My attire while painting also flows in the deviating vein from day to day, as I'm not dressing to impress. I'm not worried about whether or not some demonized church lady or some inside the beltway Washingtonian thinks I'm dapper enough. I am a primal painter.

• When I paint, I paint what I want. I take no advice from friends or foes regarding subject matter (unless of course they're paying me big money; then I'm all ears). I have no censors, editors, or elder boards telling me not to do this or that. I do what I want. It's my moment of Zen and I'm gonna milk it for me and my sanity and I couldn't give a flibbertigibbet who likes it or doesn't like it. Fortunately, a lot of people like what I have produced and have purchased many of my originals and prints. This is cool. I paint to my tastes to hang in my house. If someone buys it, fantastic. Cha-ching. If not, I'm totally cool with staring at it until I grow old and croak. You can check some of my works out at DougGilesArt.com.

• I study other artists' works. When I'm down in my studio I don't read *Investor's Business Daily*, have FOX News on, study Jeremiah, or read one of Townhall.com's blogs or … or … have Efrem Zimbalist, Jr. on reading the Bible to me via CD. Nope, my ocular-info intake is strictly focused upon fine art and the subject that I am painting, or art history books where, for instance, I'm looking at the layering techniques Rembrandt used to get the highlights on his subject's forehead. Yes, I block out my other thoughts and study art and nothing but art. I mull over Fechin's otherworldy brush strokes and palette knife work, which border on an act of God. I can sit and spend hours gazing at paintings. Give me something to sip, a nice *puros*, and a book filled with slap-your-mama-off-the-chain paintings executed by one of the masters and I won't move from that spot until I have to get up and pee. This, too, is a change from what regularly occupies my mind. Studying the who, what, when, where, and why's of the various artists who flick my switch is definitely an outcross from the subject matter I must know and master or I become unemployed.

What else do I do when I'm not hunting, fishing, or painting and I'm about to pop a blood vessel in my head?

• Exercise: I exercise for health reasons, for uncut vanity purposes, and to get the stress out of my 170-pound body. I also try to work out, as much as possible, in the great outdoors and get away from the hum of fluorescent lights and idiotic people who have somehow found a way to do squats while yellin' on their cells and forcing all within earshot to overhear exactly how crazy and tedious their lives truly are. If you're maxed out with anxiety, go to the gym, work your anxious butt out for an hour, and I guarantee you'll sleep like a baby at night versus having those regular panic attacks at 3:30 A.M.

• Sex (This applies to married couples only): One reason you might be redlining is that you're not having a regular dose of red hot relations with your spouse. (See 1 Corinthians 7:5.) Sex is a huge stress release. Keep the chase on, ladies and gents. Mix it up. Play cowboys and Indians. Life is too short to not delight in your wife's breasts, boys. (See Proverbs 5:19; Song of Solomon 1:13; 4:5; 7:3, 7-8). Do it indoors and outdoors, taunt and tease. Do it at home, abroad, in the car, in the ocean. Get jiggy with it. Buy *The Joy of Sex* and take the next year to try out everything in the book.

• Entertain: We throw a lot of parties at my house. My wife is the quintessential hostess. My daughters invite their friends and we have our buddies over and we sing, dance, shout, eat, drink, and laugh for hours at a time in the warmth of our home. Here's a caveat: make sure you invite cool people to your house and not whacked-out downers who'll suck the life out of the atmosphere.

> *If the axe is dull and he does not sharpen its edge, then he must exert more strength. Wisdom has the advantage of giving success.* (Ecclesiastes 10:10, NASB)

Solomon said if the axe is not sharp you have to exert more effort. Diversionary interests sharpen an individual. The same old, same old, causes one to become hellish, dull, and zaps our strength and drains our joy. For me, having a change of atmosphere by hunting and painting; having the poison sucked out of my system through exercise; regular doses of romance with my lady; and a nice steak, stogie, and a glass of wine, sharpens my axe and makes it easier for me to tackle the monsters in the path of my holy pursuits.

I suggest you get serious about getting joy in your life, finding a passion that has nothing to do with what you vocationally do, while exercising, entertaining, and enjoying your mate. These simple little things will help you to keep going when you start going through hell.

Chapter Six

From Crappy to Happy

[PAIN] REMOVES THE VEIL; IT PLANTS THE FLAG OF TRUTH
WITHIN THE FORTRESS OF A REBEL SOUL. —C.S. LEWIS

Life can suck. (If you don't believe me, watch Brett Michael's show *Rock of Love II: Road Trip*.) Christianity, which Jesus said was to be characterized by "life and life more abundantly" (John 10:10, KJV), can, through no fault of God's (and purely through us), really, really, suck if it is reduced to stale rote by dead denominations. And non-denominations. Sorry, non-denom guys. I nearly left you boys out. Whew. Okay, I feel better now.

Nothing sucks worse than lifeless, dour, boring, blah, blah, blah, kill-me-now religion. I would rather have Ben Stein repeatedly read to me the instruction manual of a hinge, in Latin, all day long, as a slow drip of acid rain plops repeatedly down upon my head, gradually eroding my skull cap, and eating away what's left of my brain as I sit in a diminutive and dank opossum-infested cell, lined floor to ceiling with posters of Bill and Hillary Clinton making out than to be a part of a church that reduces life with God to the exhilaration one would experience by watching paint dry.

Bueller, Bueller, Bueller, Bueller, Bueller …

Life with God, FYI, is not supposed to suck. Sure, it's not going to be a non-stop, 24/7, The Price Is Right Showcase Showdown, but it is, in all its highs and lows, a satisfying and bracing God/Man exchange.

When this redneck reads the Scripture, I see Christians living out a grand, worthwhile, risky, rewarding, supernatural schlep that cheeringly transforms them and nations. Yep, via the Christ-connection, the sinner gets to be a happy part-and-parcel of an ongoing cosmic war where souls are transferred from the dominion of Satan to the dominion of God, where the impossible becomes possible, where wrecked and messed up lives are mysteriously transformed by the power of the Holy Spirit, where sucky and crappy are never, ever heard or used in conjunction with what it means to experience God.

However, mission control, we have a problem. The postmodern conundrum is: If you look at a lot of believers they are not happy in God; but sappy, sad, slapped sods.

> I do not praise you, because you come together not for the better but for the worse. (1 Corinthians 11:17, NASB).

Unbelievable text there, folks! Paul said the Christians in Corinth were becoming worse and not better. They were becoming crappy versus happy. How many people have you seen in church lately that Christ and His people haven't changed one bit?

Their marriages are crappy.

Their kids are crappy.

Their finances are crappy.

Their health is crappy.

Their jobs are crappy.

Their sex life is crappy.

Their attitude is crappy.

Their knowledge of sound doctrine is crappy.

Their evangelism is crappy.

Their cultural kingdom influence is crappy

Their overall effectiveness for God and Christ is ... sappy, non-happy, slappy, dappy, yappy, and crappy.

Many "saints'" lives do not mirror the amazing exploits, attitudes, and actions that the Bible touts are commonplace for the Christian who's truly plugged into the divine outlet.

Yep, instead of an abundant, happy life, we see folks who call themselves believers in the Most High God existing like lifeless clods eking out a monotonous, mundane, life of quiet desperation, their lives characterized by minutia-laden minutes which turn into hours, days, weeks, months, and years. They do more for the Antichrist by their sad subsistence than for Jesus Christ, by showing to the unwashed masses that if you believe in God your life will really suuuuuuuuuuuuuuuuuuuuuck!

Some of you are no doubt thinking that I'm indulging in a typical, over-the-top lambastic, napalm-drenched, Dougism screed in saying that the above characterizes a sizable chunk of the Church. Here's a little test then: quickly rattle off in your head how many believers you personally know who you righteously envy for their attitudes and actions, their gravity-defying spirit, their marriage, kids, and calling, who are shining examples of the John 10:10 promise that Jesus gave to believers.

I'll wait while you count.

You could count them on one hand, eh?

I know; it's sad, isn't it?

What's even sadder is that we've settled for a sucky religious substitute rather than demand and stand for the real deal namely, a vibrant, gratifying, in fifty-different-ways-exchange, by following a very unpredictable, terrible, gracious, and supernatural triune God. Yep, boys and girls, some settle for crappy Christianity vs. happy Christianity.

Not me, girlfriend. Sure, Christianity is fraught with brutal trials, both physically and spiritually, but the Christian who has tapped into the God of Heaven, even in the less-than-chipper times, has an impishly confident overcomer's grin on his face knowing that the fat lady has not sung, and no matter what kind of hell-storm they go through, Christ will uphold them and make them rock in a hard place. *Sad* and *crappy* are not a part of the warrior's vocabulary or mentality. They were not true for King David, either.

So, how did dudes like David, who went through life's colon without complaining like a little chick, do it? He experienced vicious attacks by friends and foes. He committed adultery, had a man murdered, lost a son at birth, his daughter was raped by his son, and his other boy attempted a coup on his kingdom. I think that little list qualifies as crap, don't you?

What did David do? Did he settle for that slop? Did he say, especially in the attacks that came to him as a result of his sin, "Oh well, I deserve this"? What did Jesus' fleshly great, great, great (for twenty-eight generations) grand-pappy do when the crappy came? He fought against it, that's what. He didn't settle for it. He didn't allow others, or even God, to hammer him excessively without making a big noise about not liking it. He cried out for the happy place when he was having crap shoved in his face.

Here's the lesson for today, my babies: if you're in the crap zone you must cry out to get out. Literally. No silent prayers. No nicey "Now I lay me down to sleep" slop. It's time to get real and raw if you want to move from crappy to happy. You must get serious if you want to get happy.

Yep, if you're going through hell and you want God, not Obama, to bail you out, you cannot—I said, cannot—play. You must cease pretending to yourself and others that you're okay. I see this smack in church constantly. Everybody is okay, everyone is doing great, and you and I both know that most of the "I'm doing fine" retorts are more gaseous than Al Gore's gobbledygook on global warming.

If you're not doing fine and you say you're doing fine, you can actually get to the point where you believe that your haggard, toady place in life is okay, and you settle for a stupid life of quiet desperation. Jesus didn't say that He came to give you misery and misery abundantly. He said He came to give you life. Now if you're experiencing death, and what you're doing sucks like an airplane toilet, you had better come clean and tell God that your life stinks and you want that happy, satisfying stuff that Jesus promised ... or you're neva gonna get it.

David didn't settle for the crappy life his enemies or sins afforded him. Why didn't he? Well, he could read and he read in Deuteronomy and many other places in the Bible where it said that God had a higher, better way; a holy upgrade was available; and that it trumped the bogus stuff he was presently paddling through.

Look, if you've been married four times, are hooked on Asian midget porn, the girl you're currently dating is a Kazakhstani hooker, you just lost your house to foreclosure, and four irate incubuses showed up at your place last night while you were asleep, then you are not doing fine. That ain't fine. Okay? You're messed up, dawg. And as long as you: a) pretend (or worse) b). settle—then you need to clear your throat and say hello to crappy instead of happy.

David, the teenaged lion, bear, and giant killer who became king, lived more life in a week than most Christians do in a lifetime, and would not and did not tolerate the crappy when it came. He did not think it was normal and, therefore, tolerable. He didn't think, "You know, I should be living in a cave, hounded by men, and continuously punished by God." Even after his major *faux pas,* he would not, did not, settle for crappy, but only happy in God.

This Is How You Do It

People have said over the years that there are two things you never want to see made—laws and sausage. I'd like to add a third to that list, namely Christians. Watching God process a believer from a dweeb to a dynamo is about as much fun as watching Janet Reno riverdance in a tutu. Actually, that would be fun. Never mind, you get my point that it is a nasty process. That's been my pastoral reality.

I know via Christian television that most Christians appear to be shiny, happy people; veritable game show hosts with doves and fish stickers plastered everywhere. But the truth of the matter is that minus the grace of God, we're goofy, radically corrupt miscreants who'd better get raw and honest about our proclivities or we're not going to get free from the hell we're in.

If one truly wants to escape the devil inside, then raw honesty, especially in prayer, is a must. I recommend getting brutally honest before God. King David did. His prayers weren't little now-I-lay-me-down-to-sleep ditties. David's prayers were frank and rugged outcries from a man who made no bones about the smack he was dealing with both internally and externally.

He got raw and real and didn't say he was doing fine when he wasn't. Again, if you want to move from crappy to happy, you gotta cease the pretentious stuff.

This is how David did it.

Please, God, no more yelling, no more trips to the woodshed. Treat me nice for a change; I'm so starved for affection. Can't you see I'm black and blue, ... in soul? God, how long will it take for you to let up? Break in, God, and break up this fight; if you love me at all, get me out of here. I'm no good to you dead, am I? I can't sing in your choir if I'm buried in some tomb! I'm tired of all this—so tired. My bed has been floating forty days and nights on the flood of my tears. My mattress is soaked, soggy with tears. The sockets of my eyes are black holes; nearly blind, I squint and grope. Get out of here, you Devil's crew: at last God has heard my sobs. My requests have all been granted, my prayers are answered. Cowards, my enemies disappear. Disgraced, they turn tail and run. (Psalm 6, MSG)

Herewith is a crude exposition of how David blew through the rubbish in his life. I figure if it worked for David it just might work for us. Also, please note that God didn't spare His beloved from going to the "woodshed" of sucky, soul-thrashing discipline.

First off, the text gives no indication when David penned this painful poem, but the internal evidence does give us a few clues as to when he jotted down this inspired Psalm. Here are the clues as to when this was written: a.) God is beating his backside (as in black and blue); b.) people are trying to kill him. The only time I know of in 1st and 2nd Samuel and Chronicles where God and man are after David's hide was after he shagged Bathsheba and had her husband Uriah offed. Those two little lapses in judgment created a divine and human tsunami that permed his hair. Davey was in the "God's ticked at you, your enemies and friends don't like you, and your dog even thinks you're a jackass" vortex. How would you react if you were in David's sandals? Throw a pity party? Roll up into the fetal position and cry like a bebe? David said, "Help! I'm sorry! Lesson learned! Enough is enough!"

What I find interesting, if I'm right with the dating of this Psalm (and I am nearly always right; just ask my wife), is that David, with full knowledge that he brought on this private hell via his infidelity and murder, still cries out to God to get him out of the punitive spiritual and physical pit he righteously should be in.

Did he cry out for deliverance because he was a petty narcissist who didn't want life to spank him when he sinned, or was it because he understood the grace of God in the midst of the most God-awful situations? I believe it was a little of both; I mean, he was only human, right? That's my opinion; I could be wrong.

Whatever the motive was for David's "cease and desist" Psalm, one thing is clear: David is in a crappy place with God and man and he's not going to take this lying down. A broken relationship with *Yahweh* and a life of being badgered by godless hordes is not the Deuteronomical dream of bliss promised in the Pentateuch. Therefore, David yanks the parking brake on his crappy situation and bellows out for God to take him back to Happytown.

Check it out:

1. David is in the woodshed. The "woodshed," for the undisciplined punks not familiar with the term, is an antiquated word that denotes a place of trouble and chastisement for those who have behaved badly. In the woodshed, the parent would apply the board of education to the seat of knowledge, attempting through pain to wake the untoward turkey up from continuing down the path of putrification.

Yes, Dinky, in the Bible God had no problem whatsoever taking his kids down a few notches for being rebellious doofs. This experience of discipline was joyless; one could say a veritable "crappy" occurrence for the rebel soul. David said this discipline included getting yelled at, getting his soul bruised, losing the ability to sing (he was a songster), and being brought close to death. Yep, folks, he's about to pass out under what God is putting him through. So, what does David do? Well, I'm glad you asked.

2. "Treat me nice." Even though God is allowing life to thrash David, the son of Jesse doesn't forget the revelation that

God has a soft side he can appeal to. As much as God is a butt-beater when we're bad, He is also a merciful and loving God when we stop being stubborn flesh lovers.

<u>Exercise number one:</u> If you feel like you are currently being hammered by God and life more than a loose board during a Three Stooges skit, simply stop what you're doing right now and pray what David prayed, namely, "God, treat me nice." Yes, it can be that easy.

3. "Let up." I dig David's boldness right here, ladies and germs. David is righteously and justly getting what he deserves for his sins (actually, less than deserved). The Levitical penalty for what he did required David's death. David, the adulterer and murderer, tells a just and holy God to let up. Pretty ballsy, folks. A sinful, covenant-breaking, puny man tells a holy, holy, holy God to dial it down.

<u>Exercise number two</u>: Stop reading if you're currently taking a beating and tell God, if you will, reverently of course, but with earnestness, to let up. Tell him, *"No mas, Senor."*

4. "Break in." Not only does David ask for mercy and for God to stop stomping on his skull, he also asks God to break in and intervene against the human element of his butt-kicking and sort these physical enemies out. This is beautiful boldness, folks. Love me, hold me, and jump in and kick some major Philistine butt, David courageously screams. David is not stopping at two or three requests, i.e., adore me and tickle me. Oh, no. David is asking the God he has offended by his wicked, sinful behavior to not only quit beating him and start treating him nice, but in addition, to fly into his situation like Zach Thomas and clean his enemy's clock.

<u>Exercise number three</u>: Stop reading and simply pray for God to personally plow into your screwed-up-to-the max situation and route every demon and debacle you're currently dealing with.

5. "Get me out." Again, this is sa-weet. David got himself into this crappy caldron and now he is asking God to get him out. For sincere Christians, this is a difficult thing to ask. Why is it a tough request for the righteous? Well, they're honest and upright and they don't want to bug God asking Him for favors when they have been a bugger, that's why. Earnest followers of Christ are content to take life's lashings for being bellicose towards God's will and ways. In other words, it's hard for them to ask for His hand right after they bite it. I, personally, think this is cool, even though it is wrong.

In this licentious day where people walk all over the grace of God, sin with impunity, blow *Yahwe*h off like Beyonce would a broke, ugly, zit-faced, male dork with violent halitosis, get themselves in the most outrageous BS, and then have the audacity to ask God for a bailout. They have no intention to ever, ever change their behavior and you know, you just *know*, that after God bails them out, they're going to go back and eat their vomit again, and they still ask God for a get-out-of-jail-free card and expect Him to spring them, as in right now!

David, however, was not a dipstick like the grace abusing, pseudo-saints of modern evangelicalism. When David sinned he owned it, groaned it, and bemoaned it. It was not a light thing for him to sin against God. Thus, when David asked God for an out, he had zero intention of jumping back in.

<u>Exercise number four</u>: Ask God to get you out of the hell you're in. Since you're a product of postmodern, selfish "Christianity," you should also suspect the motive of your request is selfish and ask for, in addition to the extrication from the current situation, that He also give you a spirit that, once you are bailed out of said nasty situation, you do not return to wallowing in the mud.

If they've escaped from the slum of sin by experiencing our Master and Savior, Jesus Christ, and then slid back into that same old life again, they're

94

worse than if they had never left. Better not to have started out on the straight road to God than to start out and then turn back, repudiating the experience and the holy command. They prove the point of the proverbs, "A dog goes back to its own vomit," and, "A scrubbed-up pig heads for the mud." (2 Peter 2:20-22, MSG)

6. "I'm tired." David endured years, I said years, of self-imposed, hell-on-Earth pain because of his sins. He was not like the tepid and feckless "faithful" of the twenty-first century who undergo a little bad goo for three or four moon phases and they are ready to renounce Christ, pierce their tongues, get a pentagram tattooed on their foreheads, and start patronizing a gentleman's club run by Anton LaVey's daughter.

David absorbed the sting of his transgressions, learned the lesson of his rebellion, and endured more disfavor from God than most Christians sucking oxygen today would even think about tolerating from Jehovah's hand. He finally tapped out and said, "I'm tired."

This is going to tick off the happy, clappy Joel Osteen-type of Christian, but God will allow the discipline of your dirty deeds to crank down on you to such a degree that you feel faint. (See Hebrews 12:5.) I've found, that when I have had God take me to the woodshed for my shizzle, it is usually when I'm tired and ready to faint that the lesson has truly been learned and God comes in for the rescue.

<u>Exercise *numero cinco*</u>: If you're thrashed and you're hanging on by a thin thread and the lesson for your bad behavior is accomplished, simply tell God, "I'm tired, Man."

So, what happened to David? Did God kill him, ignore him, or say, "Yeah, right" and sentence this repentant dude to ten more years in Crappy State Penn? No, He did not. God granted David's requests, his prayers were answered, his enemies were disgraced, and eviscerated. David, believe it or not, went from serious crappy to serious happy by the agency of getting down and dirty before God in prayer. Not pretending he was okay, not tolerating the intolerable, not making up doctrines for why his walk with God should continue to suck as bad as it did. No, David got raw-honest before God with what he was feeling and where he was, and God transported him from crappy to happy.

Chapter Seven

I Doubt, Therefore I'm Done

WE REGARD GOD AS AN AIRMAN REGARDS HIS PARACHUTE;
IT'S THERE FOR EMERGENCIES BUT HE HOPES HE'LL
NEVER HAVE TO USE IT. —C.S. LEWIS

If you're going through a hellish trial right now you're going to need more faith in the promises of God to get you out of your temporal pressure cooker than Gary Coleman needs to get a massive bump in his career. You don't need mommy, Visa, or Obama to bail you out; you need faith in God, Green Hornet.

Atheists think faith is easy, and that to have faith all that Christians must do is turn off their brains, cross their fingers, go to Christian rock concerts, watch TBN, and hope for the best.

Biblical faith—the kind that moves mountains, shields you from demonic attacks, and changes your sad situation (in hope against hope) to an amazing testimony of God's freaky deliverance in dire straits—is a tad bit pluckier than pie-in-sky, specious, tooth fairy, farcical faith that everyone has when the birds are chirping, you're healthy, and all your bills are paid.

When one begins to go through hell on Earth, the first thing to get attacked is your faith. And when your faith is gone … you are gone. Minus faith, the trial wins and you lose. Without faith the fiery darts of *el Diablo* find you without your "shield" (see Ephesians 6:16), and the next thing you know you're channeling more demons than Nicolas Cage on a double hit of acid in a Maori Shaman's voodoo sweat lodge.

Yep, the thing you need in the center of the storm is the thing that goes under assault as soon as the hell hits the fan: namely your trust in His Word. If doubt sets in when you are down and out, you become an unarmed merchant ship off the Somali Coast, i.e., a hostage to the enemy.

The Bible says the doubter should expect nothing from God. (See James 1:2-8.) Lots of nothing.

The powers of darkness will have a field day with you.

They will play hacky sack with your soul.

As stated, maintaining faith, strengthening your faith, going from one level of faith to another level of faith is difficult and far from easy, especially under duress. That's why atheists don't believe. Faith is hard and they're wussies.

When I'm speaking of faith I'm not talking about generic belief in the tenets of essential Christian doctrines. I'm talkin' about the kind of trust that brings the power of the age to come to your smelly situation that is so jacked up Oprah, Dr. Phil, Tiger Woods, Deepak Chopra, and Benny Hinn can't do a stinkin' thing to help you.

Yep, I am not speaking about a mere head nod to the Apostle's Creed, as important as that is, but a faith that fetches the funky favor of God in the foulest of conditions and accomplishes things such as "moving mountains."

And Jesus answered saying to them, "Have faith in God. Truly I say to you, whoever says to this mountain, 'Be taken up and cast into the sea' and does not doubt in his heart, but believes that what he says is going to happen, it shall be granted him. Therefore I say to you, all things for which you pray and ask, believe that you have received them, and they will be granted you." (Mark 11:22-24, NASB)

That's the stuff I'm talking about—the kind of faith that draws the supernatural power of God into our supernaturally nappy situation.

Satan hates this kind of trust.

This kind of God-tapping belief shatters his works in you and others so you can bet your now worthless 401K that Lucifer and his defeated ilk will give you every reason on the planet for you to doubt when you should stand and trust.

If you're going to stand in faith in your messed-up situation, you had better put on a cup, because it is about to get ugly.

Really ugly.

Satan will assault you with everything in his arsenal to get you to disbelieve when you should believe. To have the promises of God manifest in your life, where you are standing triumphantly on the neck of your leviathan, will not come easy. You will be attacked by all that is fleshly and demonic with tooth, fang, and claw.

Most Christians do not make it out when Satan batters their faith.

They doubt.

Start to pout.

And then …

Flake out.

Jesus didn't die on the Cross and rise from the dead to procure unto himself a bunch of fair-weather friends. He believed and obeyed in The Most Hellish of Circumstances (the Cross) and, call Him persnickety if you will, He'd like to see His people a bit more robust in the faith; therefore, He creates situations and trials which expose doubt and boost belief.

For instance …

When He went ashore, He saw a large crowd, and felt compassion for them and their sick.

When it was evening, the disciples came to Him and said, "This place is desolate and the hour is already late; so send the crowds away, that they may go into the villages and buy food for themselves."

But Jesus said to them, "They do not need to go away; you give them something to eat!"

They said to Him, "We have here only five loaves and two fish."

And He said, "Bring them here to Me."

Ordering the people to sit down on the grass, He took the five loaves and the two fish, and looking up toward heaven, He blessed the food, and breaking the loaves He gave them to the disciples, and the disciples gave them to the crowds, and they all ate and were satisfied. They picked up what was left over of the broken pieces, twelve full baskets.

There were about five thousand men who ate, besides women and children.

Immediately He made the disciples get into the boat and go ahead of Him to the other side, while He sent the crowds away.

After He had sent the crowds away, He went up on the mountain by himself to pray; and when it was evening, He was there alone.

But the boat was already a long distance from the land, battered by the waves; for the wind was contrary. And in the fourth watch of the night He came to them, walking on the sea. When the disciples saw Him walking on the sea, they were terrified, and said, "It is a ghost!" And they cried out in fear.

But immediately Jesus spoke to them, saying, "Take courage, it is I; do not be afraid."

Peter said to Him, "Lord, if it is You, command me to come to You on the water."

And He said, "Come!" And Peter got out of the boat, and walked on the water and came toward Jesus.

But seeing the wind, he became frightened, and beginning to sink, he cried out, "Lord, save me!"

Immediately Jesus stretched out His hand and took hold of him, and said to him, "You of little faith, why did you doubt?"

When they got into the boat, the wind stopped. (Matthew 14:15-32, NASB)

The above narrative is rich ... with irony.

This is some funny stuff.

Check it out.

The disciples are watching Jesus work His miracles. He's on fire this day. He's got a crowd in the thousands. The text states that there were five thousand men, and that's not counting the women and kids, so conservatively we're talking about a Miley Cyrus concert. Jesus has a stack of folks around Him and He's feeling compassionate, and when Jesus feels compassionate people get healed.

It would have been a trip to see Christ in healing mode. Can you imagine watching Him heal a leper? The dude is rotting on the hoof. His nose, toes, and ears are all falling off, his breath stinks worse than a goat's, his skin is covered with nasty pus-filled sores, then Jesus comes along and heals this dude, and now he looks like Brad Pitt. That would be something to behold.

Now, in a crowd of twelve to fifteen thousand people, you know there had to be some folks there with some serious illnesses. Def Leppard-type stuff. From hangnails and halitosis, to dandruff and demons, to cancer and cankers, Christ came in and cranked on them all, healing everyone who was ill.

That's madness, folks.

And this was the real deal.

I guarantee it didn't smack of the *faux* healing seminars put on by hell-bound, twenty-first-century Marjoe Gortners with their oh, so obvious mood music, people catchers, extreme Aqua Net-lacquered comb-overs and elaborate crapola-laden, extra long money grab "love offerings" that are fascistly taken up right after six people supposedly get healed of their bunions.

Nope, babycakes, this was the genuine article and it must have been a sight to behold watching Christ work *contra natura.* You just know that the disciples' faith levels, after watching that mass demonstration of the power of God on the material world, were shooting through the roof. Heretofore, they had seen Jesus heal one here and there, but this was the first time they had seen Him heal a rock concert.

Jesus, however, wasn't finished flexing His holy muscle that day. After that unforgettable healing drama, the people He had just healed and the rubbernecks who watched started to get a bit peckish. Since there were no Mickey D's nearby and roach coaches hadn't come of age yet, the massive crowd was in a pickle in regard to what and where they were going to eat supper. Yes, they were gettin' hungry. They were starting to hear and feel their stomachs growl and when religious people get hungry, if they are not fed and fed quickly, it can get ugly.

The disciples, whom you would assume are now fiercely faith-filled and on fire for God, tell Jesus to send these zombies home because there is just too many pie holes to fill.

This is funny, isn't it?

Let's see ... Jesus can, against nature, make a dude's leg grow, open blind eyes, and heal some old chick with severe rheumatoid arthritis, but miraculously feeding a few thousand new believers, well, that must be above His pay grade. This is according to the freshly on-fire-with-energized-faith, but now myopic, back to carnal reasoning, and stymied, unbelieving disciples.

How soon we forget.

So what does the Third Person of the Godhead do? He asks His dense disciples to bring Him the grub that they have. The Blunder Boys have five loaves of Wonder Bread and two catfish they had left over from feasting at Bob Corcorran's River Smith's restaurant.

Jesus takes what these unbelieving believers have afforded Him and He looks up to Heaven and says, "Father, how long do I have to show these idiotic disciples of Mine Our supernatural power over their natural problems? *Oy vey.* All right, rock-n-roll, Dad, multiply it and let the feasting begin. Oh, and one more request: just to drive the point home to My clueless team of apostles, overwhelm them with leftovers. In My name I pray. Amen." And with that prayer Jesus showed His boys, once again, that He could pull rabbits out of the worst of hats. Now, you'd think that after seeing Jesus heal thousands and then supernaturally feed thousands from scraps and then bury His disciples in doggie bags and leftovers for the next several weeks, His boys would be brimming over with faith in God, right?

Right?

Wouldn't you think *you* would be overflowing with faith if you just saw that holy spectacle? You just know you'd be thinking, "Holy mackerel! This Jesus dude rocks. He can do anything. You'd be Facebooking your friends, tweeting on Twitter, going to graveyards looking for some freshly dead corpse to resurrect.

Son of a monkey, I gar-ron-tee you would be on fire for the impossible.

Wouldn't you?

In this narrative Christ wasn't convinced that after all the heavenly hullabaloo that His disciples got it. He probably could still see that daft, unbelieving look of doubt in their eyes. So, evidently, Christ, not satisfied with what He was feeling from His boys, and well aware of the fickle nature of their fleeting faith, decided to crank this bad boy up a few notches and see if they would trust Him when they are the ones who need the miracle. Their faith is sky high for other people who are ill. It is up there and out there for hungry people who need magic sandwiches. However, when it is not others but themselves that need a lifeline, will they believe Him to provide it or will they revert to their default doubt mode?

So what do you think sweet and cuddly Jesus did to address this pernicious problem with His precious follower's faith?

Did He sit down and gently explain, in both the Hebrew and the Greek, with a colorful power point and video presentation, His omnipotence over the created order and how they should always look to and believe for the God thang when things are going to hell in a hand basket?

No.

Did He sit down and sing them a Michael W. Smith song—"Friends are friends forever when the Lord is the Lord of them"?

Uh, no.

Did He say, "You poor guys have had enough of having your minds being stretched like a big woman's drawers; let's go to Pita Plus, order some kebabs and spicy hummus, and chat about today's lesson"?

Wrong again, Queequeg.

According to the lost book of the prophet Shakakah, this was the dialogue and the decision that went down between the Trinity about what to do with twelve believers who were yet to believe.

And I quote ...

Jesus: "These dudes still aren't getting it. I'm going to make these fickle little doubting Thomases learn faith the hard way. What do you think, Father?"

The Father: "I like. Very nice."

Jesus: "Holy Spirit, what do you think? Are you down with this?"

The Holy Spirit: "I'm digging it."

Jesus: "So Dad and Holy Spirit, what should we do? How should we mess with them to drive the faith point home? Should we let the ground open up and swallow them alive where they are clinging for dear life to stalactites inside an underground cavern filled with liquid hot magma?"

The Father: "Nah ... we've done that."

Jesus: "What about a plague of frogs?"

The Holy Spirit: "Uh, hello; been there and done that."

Jesus: "Grasshoppers?"

The Holy Spirit: "Dude, that's so yesterday."

Jesus: "Since they're all on fire for people getting healed, what about lighting their butts up with the most violent, festering, butt-itching hemorrhoids from hell that have ever been experienced by mankind?"

The Holy Spirit: "Okay, now I'm digging the way you're thinking."

The Father: "I know, I know—let's get 'em all jazzed up about going yachting after the spiritual high they have just experienced, and as they're talking about how Jesus can do anything for those who will believe and how they will never be the same again after seeing that demonstration of power, we send a hurricane and sink their boat."

Jesus: "Fantastic idea, Pops."

The Holy Spirit: "That's brilliant. Let's let them believe they're going to drown and see if they move in mountain-moving faith or sink like a stone with doubt.

Jesus: "Great idea, Gentlemen."

The Father: "Okay, I think we're done here. Who wants a libation?" (Shakakah 12:65-69)

And with that, the earthly experiment on Christ's ecclesiastical lab rats was settled.

Check it out ...

Immediately He made the disciples get into the boat and go ahead of Him to the other side, while He sent the crowds away.

After He had sent the crowds away, He went up on the mountain by himself to pray; and when it was evening, He was there alone.

But the boat was already a long distance from the land, battered by the waves; for the wind was contrary.

And in the fourth watch of the night He came to them, walking on the sea.

When the disciples saw Him walking on the sea, they were terrified, and said, "It is a ghost!" And they cried out in fear.

But immediately Jesus spoke to them, saying, "Take courage, it is I; do not be afraid."

Peter said to Him, "Lord, if it is You, command me to come to You on the water."

And He said, "Come!" And Peter got out of the boat, and walked on the water and came toward Jesus.

But seeing the wind, he became frightened, and beginning to sink, he cried out, "Lord, save me!"

Immediately Jesus stretched out His hand and took hold of him, and said to him, "You of little faith, why did you doubt?"

When they got into the boat, the wind stopped.
(Matthew 14:22-32, NASB)

Let's recap.

The Lord of Heaven and Earth, who is omniscient and omnipotent, set His boys up to be battered by the elements to the point that they thought they were going to die.

As in drowning.

I'd rather have a bullet to the brain than suck water into my lungs. We're talkin' Davy Jones' Locker here, people. Crab bait, baby.

Jesus not only knew His boys were about to be brought to the brink of death, but He personally ordered the situation.

Now, I might have taken a bit of poetic license with the conversation regarding the Godhead's prep for this ordeal (Shakakah 12:65-69?!), but the internal evidence is clear that Jesus told them to take a little cruise and then Lord of the elements commenced to rocking their Kasbah.

I believe it was because He probably saw their giggly and cocky know-it-all, we're-just-like- Jesus attitude and that got Him a little peeved. Yep, the disciples were getting the *big head*, and their faith in Him had not changed one iota even though they had just witnessed some of the most whacked stuff ever to go down on the planet.

So from what we know in the text, He decided to get away from these plebes and get a little R&R at His mountain retreat while His entourage took the *SS Minnow* out for a three- hour tour on Lake Crap Storm.

When his twelve dandies got on board, pulled out of the marina, and got offshore far enough that they couldn't swim in, while they were hootin' it up, drinking virgin daiquiris, and singing Clay Aiken songs, Jesus said, "All right, I have had enough of this stuff. Holy Spirit, would you please start the wave machine, put it on Death-Con 10, and sink their dinghy. Yep, I'll have one super-sized tsunami for twelve dunderhead, doubting disciples, *por favor*."

Here's the deal.

His disciples believed Him to heal people. They believed Him to save and deliver the worst skanks on the planet. They now believed Him to provide catering for thousands of people from two measly fish tacos. They believed He could pull coins out of a fish's mouth. They believed He could go toe-to-toe with the Devil on Satan's turf and terms. But did they believe Him to save them when they were in the midst of one hellacious storm?

No.

They trusted Him for others and their dramas, but not their own.

They doubted.

They didn't trust.

And they began to sink and freak.

And He let them sink and freak.

He could have stopped the storm at any time, but He waited ... and waited ... and waited 'til they were almost goners, and then the Holy Torturer shows up.

Not only did they think they were history, they didn't even recognize Him when He came walking on the water to save their unbelieving backsides. They thought He was a ghost. They were probably thinking, "Not only is our boat being ripped up, but now we have a frickin' poltergeist coming to kill us." This was a Jack Sparrow nightmare, a *Pirates of the Caribbean* bad dream.

Yep, the ones who knew Him the best trusted Him the least when the seaweed hit the fan.

Christ will not have that kind of crud coursing through His follower's veins. They were going to face the most intense circumstances known to mankind after His ascension in establishing His Church on the Earth under contrary conditions. Therefore, they needed a trust in Christ that would defy gravity, defy the most difficult of circumstances, and what better way to produce faith but by generating full-on fear.

One butt-kicking storm coming up.

Jesus is not going to allow doubts to go unaddressed in those who claim to know Him best. Just as tribulation works patience, violent storms eradicate doubt and build your spiritual faith muscle like nothing else.

That's why James, who was on that sinking ship, who saw the Wave Walker coast guard them into safe harbor, who learned the trust lesson on that sucky night could say the following with clarity and conviction after his nautical nightmare:

Consider it all joy, my brethren, when you encounter various trials, knowing that the testing of your faith produces endurance. And let endurance have its perfect result, so that you may be perfect and complete, lacking in nothing. But if any of you lacks wisdom, let him ask of God, who gives to all generously and without reproach, and it will be given to him. But he must ask in faith without any doubting, for the one who doubts is like the surf of the sea, driven and tossed by the wind. For that man ought not to expect that he will receive anything from the Lord, being a double-minded man, unstable in all his ways. (James 1:2-9, NASB)

Lesson learned by Jimmy.

This thing, this storm, was all about their faith during trials. Beholding healings and a miraculous multiplication of multi-grain bread couldn't bring that same lesson to bear on the boys.

Here's the deal: we like to talk about faith, but not actually have faith. The only real way for us mortals to find out if we actually have true faith is to be put into life's blender, have God hit the *frappe* button, and then see what happens.

Our Christianity is so conditional. If everything is perfect, or close to perfect, then, hallelujah, we will believe. If things go to hell in a handbasket, then we get PO'ed and doubt the existence and/or the promises of God and become brooding babies.

However, James states that genuine, *bona fide* faith is only known and strengthened when it is pushed to the limit. You see, God actually intends for us to use all the faith stuff we read about and get taught in Sunday school outside of the stained glass walls of the church. Y'know ... in the real world, where real crap goes down. Yep, our faith, which is born in secret, is to be tested by trials so that it can be proven when things get hopeless.

When our will is crossed, when *Twilight Zone* junk comes, when we work and obey and it seems as if we're getting punished in return, the temptation to atheism or radical doubt goes through the flippin' roof. Doubt is not a little thing—a little sin—to our faith-filled *el Capitan,* and as I have illustriously shown, He will allow the worst possible scenarios to generate trust instead of anxiety.

Most Christians bow and kiss the ring of doubt instead of rail against it. Instead, they blather against God, the Devil, the situation ... everything except their doubts and fears and it is the doubts and fears that ward off the promises of God like a crucifix to Lestat. We must learn to live in faith when we want to say, "To heck with this; forget God, forget His promises, forget this slop. I'm going to go get drunk and get nekkid."

As stated, faith in the sunshine is easy. This book is about faith under fire.

I'm talking about maintaining faith when everything, for whatever reason, is jacked up and you're so mad and confused you wanna spit, smack a tourist, memorize Sam Harris' latest atheistic screed, or spend your entire afternoon burning ants with a magnifying glass.

Listen, we cannot nurse doubt when things get dismal. Solomon states in Proverbs 23:7 that as a man thinks in his heart so is he. If you're in a bad situation and you're thinking, "I'm screwed and God's not going to come through for me." Guess what? You're screwed and God's not going to come through for you.

The promises of God, folks, are designed to be believed in the bad times.

Hello.

They are for the trouble spots.

They were made for off-road usage. They're not Miatas. They are a 4WD FJ Cruisers. They're supposed to work in the mud, in the swamp, in the jungle, underwater, in a boat that's being ripped apart by a storm, in the blistering and brutal outback.

Yes, it is when you are broken, wounded, have demons hanging off you like bats, are sick, and twisted that you are to grab the *verbum Dei,* believe it versus your circumstances, and expect a ghost to come to you walking on water, if necessary, to bring your deliverance.

All the crazy and amazing stuff that God has for the Christian demands faith to appropriate. God doesn't just give His treasures to unbelieving clods. He waits to see who's got the faith before He puts forth the heavenly funkalicious stuff.

From salvation to sanctification, to healing, to obedience to His call, and success in this life, His will and His way will be difficult because the faith it takes to actuate these goodies is not natural to us. Doubt is natural. Believing circumstances is natural. Faith in the promises of God ... unnatural.

Not only is it not a part of our fleshly make-up, but we also have the forces of darkness to contend with that give us, literally, every reason in hell why we shouldn't believe Heaven's Word. That's why the Apostle Paul spoke of faith as a fight. (See 1 Timothy 1:18.)

How about this?

Instead of wondering why or how you got into the BS (bad situation) you're embroiled in, how about starting to fight against the doubts that are screaming at you right now—those doubts that say you're never going to get out of the hell hammock you're entrenched in?

Yeah, that's it.

Instead of wondering why what is happening to you is happening. Instead of wondering how long will this bad dream go on. Instead of sitting there in your sinking ship wondering what it feels like to suck water into your lungs and how weird your corpse is going to look when it finally washes up on the shore after being in the water for a week and partially eaten by carp. Set aside the doubts and fears and say, "Bring it on, mama! I'm trusting in God like never before. This storm is my test of faith. This storm will make me stronger than ever. This storm will reveal to me the promises and the power of God like never before. So sink the boat, Jesus, because I'm looking to You to wow me with what You can and will do for those who believe."

> *I love you, God—you make me strong. God is bedrock under my feet, the castle in which I live, my rescuing knight. My God—the high crag where I run for dear life, hiding behind the boulders, safe in the granite hideout. I sing to God, the Praise-Lofty, and find myself safe and saved. The hangman's noose was tight at my throat; devil waters rushed over me. Hell's ropes cinched me tight; death traps barred every exit. A hostile world! I call to God, I cry to God to help me. From his palace he hears my call; my cry brings me right into his presence—a private audience!* (Psalm 18:1-6, MSG)

Chapter Eight

The "F" Word

THE ROAD TO THE PROMISED LAND RUNS PAST SINAI.
— C.S. LEWIS

Relax, sister. I'm not talking about that "F" word. Get your mind out of the gutter. There are words that start with "F" other than "fart," you know.

The "F" word that I'm concerned with in this chapter is— drum roll, please—*faith*.

Faith is the key to keep you going when you begin to plow through "hell."

Faith crushes doubts, fears, demons, circumstances, and the silliness that seeks to hamstring the warrior in his pursuit of his Holy Grail. So, how do we get the butt kickin' and trial stompin' faith that causes one to believe in hope against hope? That question is answered by Santo Pablo in Romanos X: XVII.

> *So faith comes from hearing, and hearing by the word of Christ.* (Romans 10:17, NASB)

Sounds easy, eh?

Faith comes by hearing and hearing the Word of God.

Hmmm ...

All we have to do is hear the Word of God?

Sounds like a piece of cake, doesn't it?

Just hearing the Word?

That's as easy as strawberry pie.

Paul has got to mean something other than audibly receiving the spoken word because I know a stack of people who have heard the Word of God preached and sung for last fifteen Olympics who lose their faith once life starts to fish-slap the snot out of them.

They do not manifest faith; they instead manifest Barney Fife and proceed to coil up in the fetal position and let demons use them as a doormat. It's as if they heard the Word, but didn't hear it. Are you hearing what I'm saying?

They're kind of like me when my wife tells me something while I'm smoking a cigar and watching a Craig Boddington African hunting video. I hear her, but I'm not to listening to her. Consequently, I always get into trouble, which usually means she cuts me off for about four to six weeks. Ouch, baby. Very ouch.

Pause and meditate.

So how do we *hear* the Word of God when we are hearing the Word of God? I'll touch on that later. For now, I'd like to talk about *what* we are to hear and then a little on *how* we are to hear.

If you're going to live a life of faith, where you rule and your trial drools, then you had better have your head under the spout where the glory comes out. (I stole that phrase from a Pentecostal preacher. And I thought I was the only one who could be that abecedarian.)

Let me try this again.

A hunger and thirst for the Word of God is a must if you wish to live a life of overcoming faith. It is a must. It is not an option. The Apostle Paul says faith comes from this fountain. Faith doesn't come from just feeling positive because an intense trial will melt away all of your upbeat feelings quicker than a mid-August South Florida sun will liquefy an overly made up chick's Cover Girl.

Yep, faith is not about your being positive and chipper like some dippy cheerleader. It's deeper than that. It is about you, not your wife, not your mommy or your grandmother, but you, having a substantial, subterranean, spiritual river of the Word of God flowing through your soul that feeds and fuels your spirit when you bump up against the forces of hell.

Check it out.

A heart (not a just a head) full of the Word of God is a heart that is full of faith in God. Which means, Dinky, you have got to start devouring the Scripture if you want to walk in the power of His Spirit and not in fear. You must stockpile the Word of God the same way Elaine Benes hoarded contraceptives on *Seinfeld.*

This is easy to do.

At least it used to be easy to do when our nation could actually read. I'm going to go out on a limb here and guess that since you have made it to this point in the book, you're probably able to read, at least at the third grade level at which I write. Congrats, Slumdog Millionaire! Since you are reading these words right now, you're one of the lucky one out of four that actually made it through public school with the ability to read, right?

Right?

Say "yes."

Yes!

Excellent.

Cool.

Okay.

We have cleared that hurdle.

Whew.

You are a candidate, via the ability to read the Word of God, to live, potentially, a life of demonic defiance.

Now since it is established that you can read, let me ask thou this: are you reading the Bible? I'm talking from stem to stern, from soup to nuts, from Adam to the Anti-Christ, both widely and deeply?

Huh?

If not, you're not serious yet about plowing through your private hell when it comes.

This is where a good chunk of the Church lives. They're not serious about being a Leonidus in life. They would love to be champions; they fantasize about being George Thorogood, "Bad to the Bone" believers. They crave it, but they won't dig deep into the Scripture, do their due diligence, and mine the principles and patterns inherent within the Bible which make them players when pain and problems arise.

Yes, these dreamers want victory but they're unwilling to do the hard work of stashing the Scripture in their hearts and souls. (See Proverbs 13:4.) The Word of God, according to the postmodern wussies, is just so tedious, taxing, time-consuming, and other troubling words that begin with a "T" and anyway, *America Idol* is on and Adam Lambert's about to sing "Rocket Man" by Elton John.

Frankly, I am amazed at the biblical illiteracy amongst the Sponge Bob Square Pants, PoMo Christianettes. It is rank. Especially down here in Miami where I pastor. When I mention Moses in Miami, the Christians down here think I'm talking about the owner of the kosher deli on Sunny Isles, Moses Finkelstein. When I ask South Florida Christians to rattle off the Ten Commandments they recite to me AA's Twelve Steps. It's like I'm in a melanin-enhanced Monty Python skit.

Y'know, not knowing the promises of God is cool, I guess. That is, if you don't want to accomplish anything amazing or plow through some insane crudaciousness that blows your buddies away so thoroughly it makes them slobber their cherry Slurpees down their shirts as they ask you, "How'd you do that, dude?"

Yes, if you want to be a mediocre Christian toad, then not having a substantial battery of Bible knowledge is groovy. Go for it. Let us know how it goes for you.

However, should you be the kind of person who wants to milk the highs and lows of life for all the experiences and excitements of a summit or plummet, God-honoring existence, then you, Hercules, need the Word of God in you more than Nancy Pelosi needs a lifetime supply of Botox and syringes.

Therefore (man, am I belaboring this point), if you want to be the fire walker instead of the little weenie wonk who gets steamrolled by life's hiccups or sidelined by some punk demon, then you, *mi amigo*, had better get a Bible you can read and begin devouring it PDQ. I destroyed, through overuse, four high-dollar, well-made, leather-bound Bibles the first three years after I became a Christian. I devoured them, and it was tasty and one of the smartest things this dumb butt has ever done.

Yes, since you have decided to throttle threats and bounce back when you have been crushed, you need the Word of God's principles, lessons, revelations, and narratives shooting through your system and formulating your attitudes and actions so that Satan will not hand you your arse when the trial comes.

I've Got the Power

"For the word of God is living and active and sharper than any two-edged sword, and piercing as far as the division of soul and spirit, of both joints and marrow, and able to judge the thoughts and intentions of the heart.

And there is no creature hidden from His sight, but all things are open and laid bare to the eyes of Him with whom we have to do." (Hebrews 4:12-13, NASB)

God's Word is not normal. His book has a freaky anointing built into it. God's Word is commanding. Think about it. By His *Word* the heavens were created. By Jesus' *Word* demons were exorcised, sick people healed, the dead were raised, cussing fishermen were called to holy service, *Seinfeld* was saved from cancellation after its first mediocre season, and by His *Word* the Godhead states the obedient will triumph.

Seriously, the Word of God has a punch to it that being Tony Robbins-upbeat cannot and does not deliver.

Oprah's little ditties don't have the *dunamis* that Jehovah's *verbum* does.

> *Grace and peace be multiplied to you in the knowledge of God and of Jesus our Lord; seeing that His divine power has granted to us everything pertaining to life and godliness, through the true knowledge of Him who called us by His own glory and excellence. For by these He has granted to us His precious and magnificent promises, so that by them you may become partakers of the divine nature, having escaped the corruption that is in the world by lust.* (2 Peter 1:2-4, NASB)

Peter said that the promises of God, contained in the Scripture, are precious and magnificent and are given to us—hello, Church—for life and godliness. Yes, they help you with life and being godly. They will even cause nasty sin-riddled dorks like us to partake, in a limited way, of God's divine nature. That's whacked, folks.

Now, when Pete used the word "precious," he didn't mean they are sweet, dainty, and *aw shucks* cute, but precious as incredibly valuable in saving your backside and transforming your gross ordeal into a soul enlarging opportunity. Yep, the Word of God, in the power-over-problems sense of the word, is valued like gold, or platinum, or diamonds, or rubies, or pre-

WWII English double rifles, or British made bolt action rifles from the early part of the twentieth century, or …

Sorry, I kind of went off track there.

Anyway, the Word of God is indispensable to your standing in faith. It is gold, baby, pure gold, when you are going through hell.

With the Word of God your mind is renewed to His way (see Romans 12:1-2), His reality, His patterns and principles, which are *muy importante* because the ways in which we think are usually completely catawampus to the way God thinks when things begin to stink. Therefore, you must know it or you will blow it.

And yes, I'm talking to you.

YOU must know the Scripture like YOU know the back of YOUR hand because YOUR carnal mind, YOUR natural thoughts in collusion with the powers of darkness are going to flood YOUR gray matter with all manner of doubts as to why YOU should not believe when YOU should.

Did you notice how I capitalized "you" and "your"?

You did?

That was me shouting at you in a high pitched and angry Nepalese accent attempting to emphasize that it's *your* job to know the Word of God like a mother orangutan knows the top of her bald-headed babies' noggins.

As you build your Bible knowledge stockade, you will quickly come to learn that when the shizzle hits the fan there is not a situation that you will be faced with that the Word of God doesn't speak to directly—or indirectly via its principles and patterns. This reservoir of revelation will afford you the wisdom and power to stay afloat once you begin to surf Hades' waves. Without it, you're done.

For example:

Say you're going broke right now during this government-spawned recession from hell and yet you refuse to look to Obama or your mama to bail you out. Here are a few promises, just a few, that God gives to the faithful once they start going through a financial crap storm. With just the following four nuggets you can begin to get your soul built back up with knowledge and trust, grounded in the authority of the Scripture, that your rich Father, i.e., God, is not going to leave you schlepping around with a "Will work for beer" sign.

> *And my God will supply all your needs according to His riches in glory in Christ Jesus* (Philippians 4:19, NASB).

Paul said, *"My God will supply all your needs."* All of them. Not Obama. Not VISA. Not your mommy. Not some high interest loan shark, but God, Sling Blade. He will float your boat if you are obedient. No matter how rank the day, God has foresworn to support those who are about His business.

The $64,000 question is: Are you on the right side of God's business? If you are, then you need to quit freaking out about your finances. Run this verse about thirty times through your head and then shout it out at the top of your lungs that your God will meet your needs according to His riches in Christ Jesus. Now get off your butt and in faith, go get a job. Let this day be the last day you look to mama and MasterCard. Take a walk on the wild side of faith for your finances.

Here are three more chunks of holy cordite to load your soul with:

> *For the LORD your God has blessed you in all that you have done; He has known your wanderings through this great wilderness. These forty years the LORD your God has been with you; you have not lacked a thing.* (Deuteronomy 2:7, NASB)

For the LORD your God is bringing you into a good land, a land of brooks of water, of fountains and springs, flowing forth in valleys and hills; a land of wheat and barley, of vines and fig trees and pomegranates, a land of olive oil and honey; a land where you will eat food without scarcity, in which you will not lack anything; a land whose stones are iron, and out of whose hills you can dig copper. When you have eaten and are satisfied, you shall bless the LORD your God for the good land which He has given you. (Deuteronomy 8:7-10, NASB)

The young lions do lack and suffer hunger; but they who seek the LORD shall not be in want of any good thing. (Psalm 34:10, NASB)

My wife and I raised our two daughters in Miami, Florida, one of the most beautiful, yet perverted places on the planet. I both love it and hate it. I love it for the lifestyle it affords us. We dig the water and the weather. I hate it because this place is a veritable east coast Sin City, with higher humidity.

When we moved here several people told us that we were insane to bring our two beautiful babies to such a morally vacuous place, and I, in part, sort of agreed with them. If my wife and I were faithless, cross-eyed, spiritual dill weeds who didn't have a stranglehold on the promises of God for our children, then, no doubt, our kids probably would be vexed by Miami's Vice.

But seeing that we are not faithless, cross-eyed, spiritual dill weeds (I might be other things, but not that), but rather a *contra mundus* couple who have an entire litany of Scriptures memorized and taken to heart, which God gives to obedient parents regarding the preservation and blessing upon their offspring, we have not sweated their upbringing in this licentious locale. And you know what? The Word of God worked—imagine that!—and our gorgeous girls are now righteous and rowdy college students who never became a part of the local teen fart cloud.

In this secularized, sin-baptized *milieu*, you need faith to raise your kids in such a smut-filled environment. If you are a half decent parent, then I know you're groping for some promises that your children won't turn into Craigslist prostitutes once they turn thirteen, right?

Parental units, you want the promises of God that your kids will be protected in this hellish culture and that your household will be uniquely blessed. If that's you, mom and dad, then check these bad boys out:

> *Praise the LORD! How blessed is the man who fears the LORD, who greatly delights in His commandments. His descendants will be mighty on earth; the generation of the upright will be blessed. Wealth and riches are in his house, and his righteousness endures forever.* (Psalm 112:1-3, NASB)

> *No evil will befall you, nor will any plague come near your tent.* (Psalm 91:10 NASB)

> *He will bless those who fear the LORD, the small together with the great. May the LORD give you increase, you and your children.* (Psalm 115:13-14, NASB)

> *The house of the wicked will be destroyed, but the tent of the upright will flourish.* (Proverbs 14:11, NASB)

• SHAMELESS PLUG ALERT! If you have a little girl you must get my book, *How to Keep Jackasses Away From Daddy's Girl.* In this book, I table scores of road-tested, historically proven, can't miss principles for raising girls with a fighting spirit, discernment, a winning attitude, and a holy vision to overcome this feces-filled culture. You will learn in the one hundred and fifty finger-burning pages how to teach your daughters to fight, shoot guns, sense BS, be classy, despise anti-intellectualism, be visionaries, party without going Britney, the value of hunting and the outdoors, the importance of traditional convictions, and how to avoid the date from hell.

• If you have a son, you ought to buy my audio book, *Raising Boys That Feminists Will Hate*. Parents, if metrosexual pop culture, feminized public schools, and the effeminate branches of "evanjellycalism" lay their sissy hands on him, you can kiss your son's masculinity good-bye—because they will morph him into a dandy. To counter the organized hatred of men and masculinity that your son is facing, it's important that you, the parent, completely blow off all the smack our PC-addled culture is trying to sell you. You'll need two things to do this: attitude and inspiration. I provide the attitude while looking to the Bible for inspiration in order to help you raise your son to be a classic man and not a postmodern pantywaist. Both products are available only at my website, www.clashradio.com.

I will now continue with my amazing text.

How about if the trial that you are facing relates to an illness or a disease? As a realist, I'm all about going to the doctor. At the same time God, the Great Physician, has allotted to us promises for our infirmities.

Will everyone get miraculously healed if sick?

No.

Do I know why? That would be no, to the tenth power.

Does that dissuade me from believing that Christ can and does heal?

Nope.

I will always believe for divine help if my health goes south. Which, thanks be to God, it hasn't, and I have had great health for the last forty-seven years.

Try these mamas out.

Bless the LORD, O my soul, and all that is within me, bless His holy name. Bless the LORD, O my soul, and forget none of His benefits; Who pardons all your iniquities, who heals all your diseases; Who redeems your life from the pit, who crowns you with lovingkindness and compassion; Who satisfies your years with good things, so that your youth is renewed like the eagle. (Psalm 103:1-5 NASB)

When evening came, they brought to Him many who were demon-possessed; and He cast out the spirits with a word, and healed all who were ill. This was to fulfill what was spoken through Isaiah the prophet: "HE HIMSELF TOOK OUR INFIRMITIES AND CARRIED AWAY OUR DISEASES." (Matthew 8:16-17, NASB)

For you have made the LORD, my refuge, even the Most High, your dwelling place. No evil will befall you, nor will any plague come near your tent. For He will give His angels charge concerning you, to guard you in all your ways. They will bear you up in their hands, that you do not strike your foot against a stone. You will tread upon the lion and cobra, the young lion and the serpent you will trample down. Because he has loved Me, therefore I will deliver him; I will set him securely on high, because he has known My name. He will call upon Me, and I will answer him; I will be with him in trouble; I will rescue him and honor him. With a long life I will satisfy him and let him see My salvation. (Psalm 91:9-16, NASB)

What if sin is getting the best of you and you're sick of being a slave to a certain vice? Slip on these PJ's before you capitulate to the flesh and live a life of quiet desperation:

No temptation has overtaken you but such as is common to man; and God is faithful, who will not allow you to be tempted beyond what you are able, but with the temptation will provide the way of escape also, so that you will be able to endure it. (1 Corinthians 10:13, NASB)

For whatever is born of God overcomes the world; and this is the victory that has overcome the world—our faith. (1 John 5:4, NASB)

No weapon that is formed against you will prosper; and every tongue that accuses you in judgment you will condemn. This is the heritage of the servants of the LORD, and their vindication is from Me, declares the LORD. (Isaiah 54:17, NASB)

For sin shall not be master over you, for you are not under law, but under grace. (Romans 6:14, NASB)

What then shall we say to these things? If God is for us, who is against us? He who did not spare His own Son, but delivered Him up for us all, how will He not also with Him freely give us all things?

Who will bring a charge against God's elect? God is the one who justifies; who is the one who condemns? Christ Jesus is He who died, yes, rather who was raised, who is at the right hand of God, who also intercedes for us.

Who will separate us from the love of Christ? Will tribulation, or distress, or persecution, or famine, or nakedness, or peril, or sword?

Just as it is written, "FOR YOUR SAKE WE ARE BEING PUT TO DEATH ALL DAY LONG;

WE WERE CONSIDERED AS SHEEP TO BE SLAUGHTERED."

But in all these things we overwhelmingly conquer through Him who loved us. (Romans 8:31-37, NASB)

What about if you have blown it severely and you're wondering if God will forgive or ever use you again? Slip these goodies into your psyche:

Therefore there is now no condemnation for those who are in Christ Jesus. For the law of the Spirit of life in Christ Jesus has set you free from the law of sin and of death. (Romans 8:1-2, NASB)

If we confess our sins, He is faithful and righteous to forgive us our sins and to cleanse us from all unrighteousness. (1 John 1:9, NASB)

Therefore, confess your sins to one another, and pray for one another so that you may be healed. The effective prayer of a righteous man can accomplish much. (James 5:16, NASB)

Be gracious to me, O God, according to Your lovingkindness; according to the greatness of Your compassion blot out my transgressions. Wash me thoroughly from my iniquity and cleanse me from my sin.

For I know my transgressions, and my sin is ever before me. Against You, You only, I have sinned and done what is evil in Your sight, so that You are justified when You speak and blameless when You judge.

Behold, I was brought forth in iniquity, and in sin my mother conceived me.

Behold, You desire truth in the innermost being, and in the hidden part You will make me know wisdom.

Purify me with hyssop, and I shall be clean; wash me, and I shall be whiter than snow.

Make me to hear joy and gladness, let the bones which You have broken rejoice.

Hide Your face from my sins and blot out all my iniquities.

Create in me a clean heart, O God, and renew a steadfast spirit within me.

Do not cast me away from Your presence and do not take Your Holy Spirit from me.

Restore to me the joy of Your salvation and sustain me with a willing spirit.

Then I will teach transgressors Your ways, and sinners will be converted to You. (Psalm 51:1-13, NASB)

The aforementioned are just a smidgen; I said a smidgen, an infinitesimal fraction, a wee little taste-test of the good love God promises His people through His Word. If you do not have these deep within your soul, then like I said, when hell comes, and it will, Satan will put on his steel-toed combat boots and proceed to kick the stuffing out of you.

Guaranteed.

As a matter of fact, I highly suggest that you buy one of the several compilations of the covenantal promises various authors and ministries have put together. I was reading one last night regarding God's promises to families who follow Him and I have to tell you that even though I have been a Christian now for over a quarter of a century, I am still gobsmacked by His goodness to us goofballs. His promises are indeed magnificent and to all the skeptics who think the Bible is a bunch of bullcrap, all I have to say is what He has promised me has come wickedly to pass.

Mucho gracias, Senor Shaddai

One of the greatest covenantal lists of positive perks the obedient believer needs to have in his head when he starts to go through hell is spelled out in OMG clarity in Deuteronomy 28:1-14:

> *Now it shall be, if you diligently obey the LORD your God, being careful to do all His commandments which I command you today, the LORD your God will set you high above all the nations of the earth.*
>
> *All these blessings will come upon you and overtake you if you obey the LORD your God:*
>
> *Blessed shall you be in the city, and blessed shall you be in the country.*
>
> *Blessed shall be the offspring of your body and the produce of your ground and the offspring of your beasts, the increase of your herd and the young of your flock.*
>
> *Blessed shall be your basket and your kneading bowl.*
>
> *Blessed shall you be when you come in, and blessed shall you be when you go out.*
>
> *The LORD shall cause your enemies who rise up against you to be defeated before you; they will come out against you one way and will flee before you seven ways.*
>
> *The LORD will command the blessing upon you in your barns and in all that you put your hand to, and He will bless you in the land which the LORD your God gives you.*
>
> *The LORD will establish you as a holy people to himself, as He swore to you, if you keep the commandments of the LORD your God and walk in His ways.*
>
> *So all the peoples of the earth will see that you are called by the name of the LORD, and they will be afraid of you.*

The LORD will make you abound in prosperity, in the offspring of your body and in the offspring of your beast and in the produce of your ground, in the land which the LORD swore to your fathers to give you.

The LORD will open for you His good storehouse, the heavens, to give rain to your land in its season and to bless all the work of your hand; and you shall lend to many nations, but you shall not borrow .

The LORD will make you the head and not the tail, and you only will be above, and you will not be underneath, if you listen to the commandments of the LORD your God, which I charge you today, to observe them carefully, and do not turn aside from any of the words which I command you today, to the right or to the left, to go after other gods to serve them. (Deuteronomy 28:1-14, NASB)

It is important to have this spiritual ammo within your soul when the storms of life begin to batter you. When you have the Word of God dwelling in you richly, whatever the adverse and tense situation you are currently being boiled in, the Word of God, united with faith, will cause you to overcome when the crud comes. When our minds are renewed with the Word of God and we actually believe His reality versus the slop we're being saddled with, such trust will cause us to take on a posture of defiance in the most difficult of circumstances.

Life and death, according to Solomon, are in the power of the tongue. (See Proverbs 18:21.) I don't know about you, but when I am getting my physical ears boxed I want my spiritual ears hearing His words of wisdom and faith instead of the world's stupidity and unbelief that often spawns from even the most well-meaning humanoids.

Having now lightly covered the importance of the Scripture when you begin to scrap in the pit of life, I wanna address *how* we can hear the Word of God *when* we hear it. The writer of Hebrews said that people could read and hear the Word of God and yet not profit from it.

> *Therefore, let us fear lest, while a promise remains of entering His rest, any one of you may seem to have come short of it. For indeed we have had good news preached to us, just as they also; but the word they heard did not profit them, because it was not united by faith in those who heard.* (Hebrews 4:1-2).

The writer of Hebrews warns New Testament Christians of the danger of hearing the Word, as Israel did in the wilderness, and not profit from it because of unbelief.

Dougy-like profit.

Profit is good.

I have never profited from anything and thought, "Yecch … that sucked!"

Yes, indeed, I want to hear the Word of God in the way in which it was intended to be heard with the resultant effect being a solid trust in God that inspires faith, encourages me to take risks, and makes me stand for that which is holy, just, and good when others are caving in all around me.

So, how do we hear when we are hearing?

First of all, you have to have a sincere heart or the Word of God will bounce off you like a Slim Fast shake off a fat sister's palette. When one comes to the Word of God, in private study or in public worship, you must come humbly, hungry, honest, and open if you want to profit from the Scripture.

If you're a know-it-all dork or a selfish me-monkey who has zero intention of repenting, or you are more famished for what Madison Avenue has for you than *Yahweh*, then more than likely the Word of God is going to come off as about as inspiring as the operation handbook for a door knob. Therefore, God's not going to wow you with revelation or give you what He gave Abraham; you don't give a crap about Him, so why should God give a crap about you? He's not going to reveal himself to you, or infuse you with hell defying, Hebrews 11 kind of faith with your kind of attitude. Jesus does not throw His pearls to swine (see Matthew 7:6) and that's what you are if you approach God in such a *laissez faire* way … a pig.

A mud lovin' Wilbur.

The person who comes to God's Word with a sincere heart seeking to grow thereby is the one to whom God will make that ink on a page become the living and dynamic Word of Life.

It's that simple.

A right heart opens the spiritual ear causing the owner of that sincere heart to, by faith.…

Stand and not fall.

See the unseen.

Walk on the path of obedience instead of rebellion.

Be courageous and not cowardly.

Speak His Word and not your fear.

Work His works instead of quit and give up.

Fight and not become passive.

Inherit the promises versus the blunt end of hell's pool cue.

He who has ears to hear, let him hear. (Matthew 13:9, NASB)

Chapter 9

In Summation

So, what did we learn via this book, my children?

Well, we learned that "If You Came to Christ to be Problem-Free Then You're Dumber Than a Bag of Hammers."

We learned that Christ solves some problems and creates others.

Caveat emptor.

He's satisfying—but He's not safe.

I know the preacher didn't tell you this during the altar call, but it's a fact, Jack.

Once inside the Good Shepherd's fold our sin nature and Satan become a royal pain in the butt to our godly aspirations like never before. Temptation and demonic attacks increase.

In addition, God's wonderful plan for your life entails you growing the heck up. This can be "hellish" for the self-obsessed, me-monkey salvation egoist. Yep, God's purpose for your life will entail a brutal unraveling of yourself. There are no shortcuts to greatness/Christ-likeness, sweetie.

We learned that Jesus said in His first YouTube lecture—the Sermon on the Mount—that storms are coming to everyone, Christian or not. Note: Jesus didn't say *if* storms come, but *when* they come. I know it sucks, but that's reality. At least He gives us a heads up, eh?

Also, Jesus didn't forewarn us of mild storms on the horizon, but squalls so violent that if you aren't well founded, your house will be destroyed. According to Christ, all Christians live in a spiritual hurricane zone. Question: How have you built your life, and are you ready when hurricanes come? Because ... they *are* coming.

We learned that we have to toughen up a bit because modern evangelicals, by and large, are an emasculated group of nancy boys who make mountains out of molehills. We aren't like our scriptural forefathers who were hardy and rowdy, tough followers of a rugged God. We are wussies, pastored by wussies, who grumble and complain when something pinches our flesh. This is a problem because demons love warfare, the flesh is incorrigible, and God's demands are high and holy—and we love Pepsi. To get through hell the first thing the believer has got to do is shut up, suck it up, and grow a pair.

We learned that God's not in the least bit interested in your carnal comfort, but in His crafted character reflected in your life. Y'know ... who you are at your core, who you are when no one sees, the habits of your heart, all that stuff that gets avoided by the modern feel-good pulpits nowadays.

Being originally from West Texas and growing up around a lot of cows and crops, I learned at an early age that cow crap makes plants grow. God allowing the poop to hit the fan in our lives is the only way to produce the fruit He likey.

Jesus said in the parable of the barren fig tree that He would dig and dung it to shock it into fruit production. Understanding that God wants us to grow up into that which doesn't make Him want to puke helps us to swallow the jagged pill of temporarily getting buried in compost.

We learned that most of our pain is self-created. At least mine is. Yep, I created most of the hell in my life that I have had to go through. I'd love to blame others—even God—but if I have to be honest, I spawned most of the monsters that I have had to deal with. Yep, my rebellious nature, my past hatred for God and His ways, and my innate stupidity has blown through the checks and balances of the Word of God, the conviction of the Holy Spirit, and the communion of the saints and has landed me facedown in the mud.

There is no way I can fault God or the Devil for 99.9 percent of the stuff that has happened in my life. What about you? The key to getting out of your self-inflicted, hellish nightmare is first and foremost to take responsibility for your own ridiculousness.

We learned that, according to the Bible, saints experience "hell" because they're kicking butt and taking names for God. A righteous life does not exclude a believer from the blunt end of hell's pool cue. Matter of fact, it guarantees it!

Given this fact believers can do one of two things: one, they can fall on the floor, roll up in the fetal position, suck their thumbs, and wet their diapers; or two, they can put on the full armor of God and resist the Devil. The answer to demonic attacks is to use the spiritual weapons God has equipped us with. Can you dig it?

We learned, and I guarantee you haven't heard this ditty much in our dilatory churches, that God will, for His good purpose, toss His kids into divine darkness and inexplicable trials simply to stretch them for His own intents.

This is the purpose driven storm for the purpose driven life. In this storm you can pray, repent, bind the Devil, and go to church thirty times a week, and yet it won't go away. This "hell" is brutal in that it is not because of sin, but because of a future intended use He has in mind for the benefit of not only just you, but also others. Moses, David, Joseph, Job, and a host of folks know what I'm talking about. The key to this tsunami is to lay low, get content with His weird dealings, and just worship.

We learned as Solomon stated in the Book of Ecclesiastes that one of the keys to surviving the brutalities of life is to relax ... chill ... drink some wine ... and have a good laugh. When one begins to go through the meat grinder of life, the first thing to vanish like a pack of smokes at an AA meeting is joy.

Joy is serious business because according to God, without it you're oh, so lame. You and I won't be able to stand against the forces of hell or our rotten desires without getting happy in God. Yep, without the gravity-defying virtue of joy cranking through our spirits we won't be able to pray the fuzz off a peach. Fickle and vapid Christians disobey the command to rejoice in all things, and God means *all* things—this entails all non-yippee stuff. Consequently, they don't transcend their transient trials, and God has no other recourse but to send them around the mountain again until they learn the power of laughing their butts off in the face of adversity.

We learned that if one wants to truly escape the devil inside then raw honesty, especially in prayer, is a must. I recommend getting brutally honest before God. King David did. His prayers weren't little now-I-lay-me-down-to-sleep ditties; David's prayers were frank and rugged outcries from a man who made no bones about the smack he was dealing with both internally and externally.

We learned, and I hate to bring the Bible into this, but according to the book of James, the Christian is commanded to view trials as a gift.

A gift?

Please.

"Go sell crazy somewhere else," says the narcissistic saint of the new millennium.

The postmodern, puny, dwarf Christians only regard as gifts that which further augments their immediate wants and needs. To have something come into their lives that would rock their self-love boat is seen not as a gift, but a curse. However, according to God, that which is meant for evil can be turned into good if you realize that this little pain in the butt has come into your life to test your faith, purge your heart, and reveal God's mighty power.

My prayer is that this book has assisted to you to keep going when you start going through hell and once you've made it through hell, not to become an insensitive jerk like me. God exhorted Israel to remember that they used to be slaves in Egypt and to remember their pain. It's prudent for the believer and profitable to the Church for the person who has weathered storms not to become an unfeeling fop, but rather a *sensei* who shows others how to navigate life's tricky streams.

And lastly, don't get too comfortable or cocky just because you're currently out of a storm, because the NOAA weather system says another tropical squall is brewing out in the gulf.

Also by Doug Giles

How to Keep Jackasses from Daddy's Girl

A Time to Clash: Papers from a Provocative Pastor

God's Warriors & Wild Men: Why Men Hate Church and What to Do About It (Audio Book)

10 Habits of Decidedly Defective People: The Successful Loser's Guide to Life

Raising Boys That Feminists Will Hate (Audio Book)

The Bulldog Attitude: Get It or Get Left Behind

Ruling in Babylon: Seven Disciplines of Highly Effective Twentysomethings

Political Twerps, Cultural Jerks, Church Quirks

Available online at www.ClashRadio.com